REA's Test Prep Books Are The Best!
(a sample of the <u>hundreds of letters</u> REA receives each year)

" I did well because of your wonderful prep books... I just wanted to thank you for helping me prepare for these tests. "
Student, San Diego, CA

" My students report your chapters of review as the most valuable single resource they used for review and preparation. "
Teacher, American Fork, UT

" Your book was such a better value and was so much more complete than anything your competition has produced (and I have them all!). "
Teacher, Virginia Beach, VA

" Compared to the other books that my fellow students had, your book was the most useful in helping me get a great score. "
Student, North Hollywood, CA

" Your book was responsible for my success on the exam, which helped me get into the college of my choice... I will look for REA the next time I need help. "
Student, Chesterfield, MO

" Just a short note to say thanks for the great support your book gave me in helping me pass the test... I'm on my way to a B.S. degree because of you! "
Student, Orlando, FL

" The gem of the book is the tests. They were indicative of the actual exam. The explanations of the answers are practically another review session. "
Student, Fresno, CA

(more on next page)

" I just wanted to thank you for helping me get a great score
on the AP U.S. History... Thank you for making great test preps! "
Student, Los Angeles, CA

" Your Fundamentals of Engineering Exam book was the absolute best
preparation I could have had for the exam, and it is one of the major
reasons I did so well and passed the FE on my first try. "
Student, Sweetwater, TN

" I used your book to prepare for the test and found that the advice and the
sample tests were highly relevant... Without using any other material, I earned
very high scores and will be going to the graduate school of my choice. "
Student, New Orleans, LA

" What I found in your book was a wealth of information sufficient to shore up
my basic skills in math and verbal... The section on analytical ability was
excellent. The practice tests were challenging and the answer explanations
most helpful. It certainly is the Best Test Prep for the GRE! "
Student, Pullman, WA

" I really appreciate the help from your excellent book. Please keep
up with your great work. "
Student, Albuquerque, NM

" I used your *CLEP Introductory Sociology* book and rank it 99% — thank you! "
Student, Jerusalem, Israel

" The painstakingly detailed answers in the sample tests are the most helpful
part of this book. That's one of the great things about REA books. "
Student, Valley Stream, NY

REA's
TESTBUSTER™
for the
LSAT

Robert K. Burdette, Ph.D., J.D.
Former Instructor of English
University of Michigan
Ann Arbor, MI

Anita Price Davis, Ed.D.
Chairperson of Education Department
Converse College
Spartanburg, SC

Christopher Dreisbach, Ph.D.
Associate Professor of Philosophy
Villa Julie College
Stevenson, MD

Theodora Glitsky, M.A.
Instructor of Philosophy
Harris-Stowe State College
St. Louis, MO

Timothy M. Hagle, J.D., Ph.D.
Assistant Professor of Political Science
University of Iowa
Iowa City, IA

H. Hamner Hill, Ph.D.
Chairperson of Philosophy Department
Southeast Missouri State University
Cape Girardeau, MO

Connie Mauney, Ph.D.
Associate Professor of Political Science
Emporia State University
Emporia, KS

John E. Parks-Clifford, Ph.D.
Chairperson of Philosophy Department
University of Missouri–St. Louis
St. Louis, MO

Wesley G. Phelan, Ph.D.
Assistant Professor of Political Science
Eureka College
Eureka, IL

John G. Robison, Ph.D.
Chairperson of Philosophy Department
University of Massachusetts–Amherst
Amherst, MA

Garrett Ward Sheldon, Ph.D.
Associate Professor of Political Science
Clinch Valley College
Wise, VA

Paul C.L. Tang, Ph.D.
Chairperson of Philosophy Department
California State University–Long Beach
Long Beach, CA

REA • 61 Ethel Road West • Piscataway, New Jersey 08854
http://www.rea.com

REA's TESTBUSTER™ for the LSAT

Printed in the United States of America

Library of Congress Catalog Card Number 99-74656

International Standard Book Number 0-87891-144-8

Research & Education Association
61 Ethel Road West
Piscataway, New Jersey 08854
Email: info@rea.com

About Research and Education Association

Research and Education Association (REA) is an organization of educators, scientists, and engineers specializing in various academic fields. Founded in 1959 with the purpose of disseminating the most recently developed scientific information to groups in industry, government, high schools, and universities, REA has since become a successful and highly respected publisher of study aids, test preps, handbooks, and reference works.

REA's Test Preparation series includes study guides for all academic levels in almost all disciplines. Research and Education Association publishes test preps for students who have not yet completed high school, as well as high school students preparing to enter college. Students from countries around the world seeking to attend college in the United States will find the assistance they need in REA's publications. For college students seeking advanced degrees, REA publishes test preps for many major graduate school admission examinations in a wide variety of disciplines, including engineering, law, and medicine. Students at every level, in every field, with every ambition can find what they are looking for among REA's publications.

Unlike most Test Preparation books that present only a few practice tests which bear little resemblance to the actual exams, REA's series presents tests which accurately depict the official exams in both degree of difficulty and types of questions. REA's practice tests are always based upon the most recently administered exams, and include every type of question that can be expected on the actual exams.

REA's publications and educational materials are highly regarded and continually receive an unprecedented amount of praise from professionals, instructors, librarians, parents, and students. Our authors are as diverse as the subjects and fields represented in the books we publish. They are well-known in their respective fields and serve on the faculties of prestigious universities throughout the United States.

Acknowledgments

In addition to our authors, we would like to thank the following:

Dr. Max Fogiel, President, for his overall guidance which has brought this publication to completion.

Carl Fuchs, Director of REA's Testbuster Series, for his guidance and management of the editorial and graphic arts staff through every phase of development, from design to final production of book.

Gary J. Albert, Project Manager of REA's Testbuster Series, for his substantial editorial contributions.

Nicole Mimnaugh, New Book Development Manager, for her editorial contributions and meticulous proofreading.

Ilona Bruzda, Senior Graphic Designer, for the design, illustrations, and graphic layout of text and cover.

CONTENTS

Contents

CHAPTER 3

LSAT Practice Test   23

CHAPTER 4

Attacking the Reading Comprehension Questions   107

CHAPTER 5

Attacking the Analytical Reasoning Questions   149

CHAPTER 6

Attacking Logical Reasoning Questions   191

CHAPTER 7

Attacking the Writing Sample   221

ANSWER SHEETS   235

REA's

TESTBUSTER™

for the

LSAT

Chapter 1

Introducing REA's LSAT Testbuster

Busting the LSAT

REA's LSAT Testbuster is the result of a massive effort to provide you with the best possible preparation for the LSAT. The techniques, strategies, tricks, and tips you'll learn from this book have been tested and proven to work on the LSAT. They are the techniques and strategies used by the leading national coach and review courses. Why use a Testbuster? Because the testbusting techniques are proven, they work, and they will help you get the best score you possibly can on the LSAT.

Bust it!

If you follow the strategies we teach you, you will do better on the LSAT than you ever thought possible. "But," you may ask yourself, "Won't that mean I have to spend every spare moment I have studying the same stuff that I've studied in college?" No. The techniques we will teach you have nothing to do with the way you were taught in your undergraduate courses. We will teach you to beat the LSAT. That means we will teach you ways to beat the people who write the LSAT at their own game. There are ways to use the structure of the LSAT to your advantage. We will teach you these methods. Armed with them, you will go to the test center, sit in a desk, and take the LSAT knowing you will not be intimidated. In fact, the LSAT should be intimidated by you because you will know its weaknesses.

What is the LSAT?

Important Information!

The LSAT is taken by college seniors or graduates looking to be accepted into a law school. As you probably already know, law schools use the LSAT as a way to judge students who apply for admission. Since there are many different grading systems in colleges across the country, a professor in Oklahoma will grade differently than a professor in Maine. For law schools, the LSAT is a quick and easy way to place prospective students on equal ground. Your LSAT score, along with your undergraduate grade point average are the most important factors in determining where you finally attend law school. If you have your sights on a top law school, you'll have to work very hard on the LSAT. An LSAT score in the 90th percentile and above is the minimum for admission to competitive schools.

Who Makes the Test?

The LSAT is developed and administered by the Law School Admission Services (LSAS) under the supervision of the Law School Admission Council (LSAC). The LSAT is required by every American Bar Association (ABA)-certified law school in the United States.

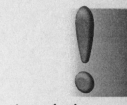

Important Information!

Beating a Multiple-Choice Test Like the LSAT

The LSAT is comprised of multiple-choice questions, with the exception of the writing sample. **The significance of a multiple-choice test is that the correct answer is always given,** in contrast to "fill-in-the-blank questions" or essays where you have to come up with the answer yourself. Of course, finding the correct answer among the multiple choices is what the test is all about.

Bust it!

Testbusting will teach you that sometimes it's easier to find the incorrect choices than the correct answer. By eliminating the incorrect choices you can hone in on the correct answer. There will be a lot more about that later.

The Sections and Questions of the LSAT

The LSAT is broken into three subjects: Reading Comprehension, Reasoning (Logical and Analytical), and Writing. You will be given about three-and-a half hours to complete six sections. The sections are broken down as follows:

Section	Number of Questions	Time
Reading Comprehension	26 to 28	35 minutes
Logical Reasoning	24 to 26	35 minutes
Logical Reasoning	24 to 26	35 minutes
Analytical Reasoning	22 to 24	35 minutes
Trial "Experimental" Section (unscored)	varies	35 minutes
Writing Sample	1 essay	30 minutes

Important Information!

The five multiple choice sections can appear in any order, but the writing sample is always last. The "Trial Section" is a group of unscored questions that the LSAS uses to try out new questions. You will not be scored on this Trial Section, nor will you be told which section it is. So do your best on all six sections.

A brief summary of the questions appear as follows:

- ## Reading Comprehension
  26 to 28 comprehension questions based on four brief reading passages (60 to 80 lines). Approximately five to eight questions will follow each passage. The reading passages and questions are not presented in any order of difficulty.

- ## Logical Reasoning
  Two sections of 24 to 26 inferential questions based on arguments (each about three to four sentences in length). Logical Reasoning questions are not presented in any order of difficulty.

- ## Analytical Reasoning
  22 to 24 questions based on four "mind teaser" puzzles. Each puzzle has a premise and conditions and the questions present tasks about the possible arrangements of the elements of the puzzle.

- ## Trial Section
  An unscored experimental section repeating one of the multiple choice sections. The Trial Section is not identified and will not be counted as part of your score.

- ## Writing Section
  A 30-minute essay on an assigned topic.

Important Information!

Don't worry about the types of questions too much right now. We'll go into further detail about each type of question you'll encounter on the test later on in this book.

How Is The LSAT Scored?

The LSAT gives you one point for each multiple-choice question you answer correctly. You don't lose any points if you answer a multiple-choice question incorrectly. Also, leaving a question blank does not affect your score, you neither lose nor gain points. The Writing Test is not graded and is not a part of your LSAT score. A photocopy of your essay is sent, unmarked, to each law school that receives your score. We'll discuss the Writing Test in more detail in that chapter.

Scoring the Test

The number of questions you answered correctly in each section are added together to reach your raw score. This raw score is then converted to a scaled score. The scaled score is set on a scale of 120 to 180, with 180 being the best possible score.

When you receive your scores from the LSAS, you will see a scaled score and a percentile ranking. This ranking compares your performance with the scores other test-takers received on the LSAT for the previous five years. If a scaled score of 150 is the average LSAT score, and you received a score of 150, your percentile ranking would be 50. If you received a higher score, say 156 then you would leap up to a ranking of about 70. This would mean you scored higher than 70 percent of the people who took the LSAT in the last five years. See pages 26 and 27 for Scaled Scores and Percentile Ratings from Recent LSATs.

Your LSAT score is a very important factor, if not THE

MOST important factor, when you apply to law school. While not the only factor considered by law schools, your LSAT score, along with your undergraduate GPA, is the most critical factor to determine whether or not you are accepted into a law school. Unlike undergraduate programs, law schools don't put a lot of emphasis on your extracurricular activities or how you performed in interviews. An above-average writing sample on the LSAT can be favorable, but it won't make up for a mediocre LSAT score (or may make no difference at all). Since you've already completed your undergraduate courses (or at least most of them), there isn't very much you can do about your GPA. So the most proactive step you can take to ensure you are accepted into the law school of your choice is to prepare yourself to attack the LSAT to get the highest score you possibly can. And that is just what this book has been designed to do for you.

How Should I Study for the LSAT?

It is very important for you to choose the time and place for studying that works best for you. Some people will set aside a certain number of hours every morning. Others may choose to study at night before going to sleep. It doesn't matter when you study, it only matters that you study every day. You will not help yourself by trying to read this entire book the night before you take the LSAT!

Study Schedule

The study schedule that we provide on the next page is designed to help you prepare for the LSAT in a flexible time frame. The schedule presented is for an 8-week study course. However, you can condense it to a 4-week program by combining two weeks of studying into one. Remember, the more time you spend studying, the more prepared and relaxed you will feel on the day of the exam. If you choose to follow the 8-week schedule, plan to spend about an hour a day studying for the LSAT.

It is very important that you give yourself the best possible chance to learn the techniques that this book offers. This means studying in a distraction-free environment. You should not have a radio or TV on while you are studying. Try to find a space where no one will interrupt your studying. Give yourself lots of light and space to spread out. A poorly lit room will strain your eyes and make you tired before you finish studying for the day.

Two-Month Study Schedule

Study Schedule

Week	Activity
• **Weeks 1 & 2**	*Read and study the introduction to this book. Then, take the Practice Test to determine your strengths and weaknesses. Carefully study the detailed explanations for the questions you answered incorrectly. Make sure you understand why you got each question wrong. Pay attention to sections where you missed a lot of questions. You will need to spend more time reviewing these sections.*

- **Week 3**   *Study the review on the Reading Comprehension Questions and answer the drill questions. Review any material that you answered incorrectly in the drills.*

- **Week 4**   *Study the review on Logical Reasoning Questions and answer the drill questions. Review any material that you answered incorrectly in the drills.*

Study Schedule

- **Week 5**   *Study the review on Analytical Reasoning Questions and answer the drill questions. Review any material that you answered incorrectly in the drills.*

- **Week 6**   *Study the Writing Sample review and answer the drill essay. Since the Writing Sample will not directly affect your score, review this chapter only when you have a firm grasp on the other LSAT sections.*

- **Weeks 7 & 8**   *Take the Practice Test again. Compare the score you received on this practice test to the first test you took. Be sure to look for areas where you missed a lot of questions. Review the areas where you missed a lot of questions. Take your time and relax. Cramming won't help you.*

Chapter 2

The Most Important Strategies for Beating the LSAT

Don't Be Intimidated!

The single most important strategy you can use to beat the LSAT is NOT TO BE INTIMIDATED. Test-taking anxiety, a very common factor when students sit down to take the LSAT, can absolutely ruin your score. You've already learned that there are ways to beat the LSAT by using its weaknesses against itself. And you've already learned what types of questions to expect to see on the LSAT. **You already know a lot about this test and you haven't really even begun to study for it!** So just remember, knowledge is power. DON'T BE INTIMIDATED!

Bust it!

Your Best Friend: The Process of Elimination

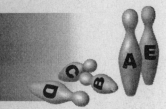

Eliminating Answer Choices

You probably already know how to use the process of elimination, but you may not realize it. More than likely, you've been taking multiple-choice tests for years. And you've been using the process of elimination to help yourself out while taking those tests. Let us show you:

Say you've been asked the following question on a history test (lucky for you there are no history questions on the LSAT!).

Who was the 12th president of the United States of America?

(A)   Bill Clinton

(B)   Zachary Taylor

(C)   Gerald Ford

(D)   Thomas Jefferson

(E)   Franklin D. Roosevelt

Now, you may not know the order of presidents, but we bet you could still get the correct answer. Lets looks at answer choice (A). You know that Bill Clinton is the current president of the United States. You probably even know that he's the 42nd president. So you know this choice is incorrect.

Answer choice (B) may be tough for you, so we'll go on to the next choice.

Gerald Ford, answer choice (C), was president pretty recently and you should know that. There have definitely been more than 12 presidents before Ford, so you can safely assume that answer choice (C) is incorrect.

You probably know that Thomas Jefferson was one of the United States' first few presidents. In fact, it is likely that you know that Jefferson was the 3rd president. You can easily label answer choice (D) as incorrect.

The final answer choice, Franklin D. Roosevelt, may give you some difficulty. You may know that he was president during World War II. You probably can say with confidence that Roosevelt couldn't have been the 12th president just by knowing he served during the 1930s and 40s, but a bit of math will tell you for sure. If World War II was fought in the 1940s, that means about 150 years had passed since the first president in 1790. Dividing 150 by 4 (the number of years in a presidential term) and you get a little over 37. There is no way that Roosevelt could have been the 12th president. This is an incorrect answer choice.

Eliminating Answer Choices

There, see how easy that question was! You figured out that Zachary Taylor was our 12th president without knowing the exact order of presidents. That's using the process of elimination!

"But," you're probably thinking to yourself, "that's not the way I've been taught in school to get the answers." You're absolutely correct. Your teachers and professors want you to work through each question very carefully and using all your knowledge. But guess what? The LSAT doesn't care how you got the right answer, it only cares that you filled in the correct oval on your answer sheet! And using the process of elimination will help you fill in the right oval more times and faster than if you tried to work through every question like your teachers want you to.

Eliminating Answer Choices

Now, we don't want to make you believe that every question on the LSAT is going to be as easy to answer as the one we just showed you. Because they aren't. But by using the process of elimination, you can usually eliminate 3 of the 5 answer choices. This means you've taken a 1 in 5 chance, or 20% chance, of getting the correct answer and turned it into a 1 in 2 chance, or 50% chance, of getting the correct answer! That sounds pretty good, doesn't it?

But wait! Say you use the process of elimination on 20 questions. That means you have a 50% chance of getting the right answer for those 20 questions (if you've eliminated 3 of the 5 choices). If you get 50% of the questions right, that means you've earned 10 points for the 10 correct answers (50% of 20 is 10). "Yes," you're saying, "but what about the 10 questions I got wrong?" Well, you lose a quarter of a point for getting the 10 questions you answered wrong. Which means you lose 2.5 points. But that means you've earned more than you've lost! The process of elimination gave you 7.5 points for free!

Just Fill in Those Ovals!

Another very important strategy in beating the LSAT is to blindly guess. That's right, if you can't answer the question, and can't use the process of elimination to reach the correct answer, just pick a letter and fill in the oval!

"How can this be true?" you're probably asking. "Don't I lose points for getting the wrong question?" No, you don't! If you guess the wrong answer NOTHING HAPPENS; you don't gain or lose points. However, if you guess the correct answer, you gain a whole point! Let's look at this in more detail:

By applying this idea of blindly guessing with the law averages, you can expect to get 1 in 5 answers correctly (by blindly guessing we mean you don't even look at the questions and answer choices, but guess the same letter choice over and over again!). What? Well, since there are 5 answer choices given for each LSAT question, you can expect on average to guess the correct answer 1 out of 5 times (read up on your mathematical probability if you don't believe us!). This means that by guessing 5 times you'll get 1 question right (as long as you pick the same letter choice every time you blindly guess).

So you now see that blindly guessing will not affect your score on the LSAT—it can only improve it!

By now, you've probably already reached our next conclusion: "We're playing the law of averages, if I blindly guess along with using the process of elimination I'll beat the odds." Right! If you blindly guess you have a 1-in-5 chance of getting the question right. As you already learned, if you eliminate just 1 answer choice you increase your odds of getting the right chance from 1-in-5 (20%) to 1-in-4 (25%). This means that if you blindly guess on 20 questions, you can expect to get 4 answers correct. If you eliminate just 1 answer choice from those same 20 questions and blindly guess from the remainder of answer choices, you can expect to get 5 questions correct. (This doesn't apply if you've eliminated the letter choice you've been using to blindly guess, but you are still increasing your odds of getting a correct answer). So, when used together with some process of elimination techniques, guessing on the LSAT will drastically raise your score!

We'd like to show you another reason guessing at a question is better than leaving it blank (as if getting a better score isn't enough!). Some people wrongly believe that if you answer a dozen questions correctly and leave the rest blank they will receive a perfect score. This is absolutely wrong. While it is true that points are not deducted for leaving questions blank, you don't gain points either.

Should I Guess?

"How does this apply to guessing," you're probably asking. Well, you need to answer every question on the LSAT correctly to earn a perfect score of 180. If you leave one question blank, you can only get a 172 or 173. If you leave 20 questions blank, the best score you can get is a 160. This means there is a penalty for leaving questions blank. And once you lose those points, you can't make them up later on in the LSAT where you're skills are stronger. So guessing an answer will also help you to avoid losing points on the LSAT!

Use Your Time Wisely

The LSAT is a timed test. You'll be given 35 minutes to work on each section (and 30 minutes for the Writing Sample). You'll need to work steadily, concentrating very hard on the questions. In fact, the LSAT is designed so the average test-taker won't be able to get to every question in the time allotted.

Some people would think that the best way to attack a test that is designed to prevent you from getting to every question in the allotted time is to rush through each question to at least get a look at all of them. THIS IS WRONG. If you were to employ this technique you would not be spending enough time on each question to answer it correctly. The LSAT is designed so that you must read each question and its choices closely—you won't be able to quickly look them over and get the correct answer. The correct strategy is to slow down and make sure you answer fewer questions with more accuracy.

If you begin a question and quickly become confused, skip it and move onto the next question. Mark the question in your test booklet and go back to it if you have time left over. **The questions on**

Watching the Clock!

the LSAT are NOT presented in order of difficulty. The most difficult question in a section could be the first one. You would be wasting valuable time by trying to work through this first question only to find that you don't have the time remaining to work out questions that are easier (which you have a better chance of answering correctly). **If you are having difficulty understanding or answering a question, immediately move on and look for a question you can answer with some degree of confidence.**

Watching the Clock!

It is common for someone who takes their time, spending more time with fewer questions to answer more questions correctly than someone who rushes to get to every question. If you slow down and answer only 75 percent of the questions, you'll get more questions correct than if you quickly tried to answer all 101 questions on the LSAT.

But there's a bonus! If you only answered 75 percent of the questions, you would have 25 or 26 questions you couldn't get to. But, as we discussed previously, if you blindly guess at these 25 or 26 questions, the law of averages says you'll get about 5 of them right! (as long as you fill in the same letter choice for every answer you guess!). And 5 correct answers will bump up your scaled score by about 3 or 4 points. And that would increase your percentile ranking by almost 10 percent!

So, not only will slowing down and answering fewer questions allow you to get more correct answers than rushing to answer all 101 questions, but by blindly guessing on a question you didn't get to will enable you to improve your score! A double-bonus!

So, don't worry about getting to all of the questions. Instead, skip the hard questions and concentrate on the questions you can answer to ensure that you choose the correct answer. And just before you run out of time, go back and fill in the blank ovals on your answer sheet (using the same letter choice for every answer) because you know that guessing will only help your score.

Don't Look At The Directions!

Important Strategy

The LSAT is a standardized test. That means the directions and the types of questions will be the same from test to test, person to person. If you learn the directions and how to approach each type of question before your test day, you will save valuable time by NOT reading the directions before beginning to answer the questions. And as you've already learned, time is critical on the LSAT. Also, knowing what to expect and how to handle all the question types on the test will enable you to avoid test-anxiety and nervousness.

You Paid For It, Use It!

Important Strategy

Our final tip for beating the LSAT is to write in your test booklet. You've paid to take the LSAT and your test booklet will be thrown away as soon as you hand in your answer sheet. So scribble in it, mark it up, make notes to yourself...do whatever you want!

One of the best ways to use your test booklet is to mark questions that you've spent some time on but decided to skip. By marking these questions, you can go back to them if you have time left over.

When answering questions, cross out answer choices you know you're not going to select. By crossing them out while using the process of elimination, you will avoid wasting time by reading and re-reading choices you've already eliminated. This economy of time will easily earn you more points throughout the LSAT.

Summary of the "Must Do" Testbusting Rules

✔ **Don't Be Intimidated**

Fear is your worst enemy. Studying this book will enable you to approach the LSAT with confidence and poise.

✔ **Use the Process of Elimination**

Possibly the easiest and quickest way to increase your score. Eliminating answer choices will lead you towards the right answer.

✔ **Guess, Guess, Guess**

Can't seem to get the answer? Pick a letter (use the same letter for every question) and fill in that oval! If you blindly guess you'll get 1 answer in 5 right, but use the same letter consistently when you can't eliminate any of the answer choices. If you can eliminate just 1 answer choice, you'll get 1 answer in 4 right. Either way, you'll raise your score because leaving an answer blank will cost you points that you can't make up later in the test.

✔ **Use Your Time Wisely**

On Target!

Answer fewer questions with greater accuracy. Don't rush to get to every question, this leads to careless mistakes and costs points. The LSAT is designed so the average test-taker won't have time to get to every question. So pay attention and make sure you answer the questions you can get to correctly. Remember the questions are not presented in order of difficulty. If you find yourself having trouble understanding or answering a question, mark it and move on to a question you feel more comfortable with. Then go back and guess the correct answers for the questions you couldn't get to (making sure to use the same letter choice for every answer you guess). This is a double-bonus in your score: more correct answers than if you rush through every question and a 1 in 5 chance of selecting the correct answer for a question you couldn't get to.

✔ **Don't Look At The Directions**

Why waste time reading what you already know? Learn the directions before hand and ignore them during the test.

3

LSAT Practice Test

Now that you have some background information concerning the LSAT, you are ready to take the practice test. This test is designed to help you identify where your strengths and weaknesses lie. This will help you make more effective use of your study time.

This is a full-length test, so you should try to simulate actual testing conditions as closely as possible. Allow yourself three hours to complete the test. Situate yourself in a quiet room so that there will be no interruptions and **keep track of the time** allotted for each section.

LSAT
Practice
Test

After you complete the practice test, identify your strengths and weaknesses by scoring each section of the test. The next step is to study the reviews and answer the drill questions in each chapter. Then, after studying the reviews, take the practice test again and see how well you score.

There are other options, however. The first option is to take the practice test and study only the reviews in your weaker areas and then retake the test. A second option is to study all the reviews and answer all the drill questions first. Then take the practice test and go back and review your weaker areas. You may already know where your weaknesses lie and might want to read the reviews and answer the drill questions for those sections and then take the test.

Remember to employ all of the Most Important Strategies for Busting the LSAT which we introduced in Chapter 2. Begin using these strategies now so you can become comfortable with them before taking the actual LSAT.

It is a good idea to photocopy the answer sheets for the practice test, even if you do not plan on retaking the practice test. By photocopying the answer sheets, you will ensure that you will have clean answer sheets no matter how many times you take the practice test.

SCALED SCORES AND PERCENTAGES FOR THE LSAT

Conversion Chart

For Converting Raw Scores to the 120-180 LSAT Scale

Raw Score	Expected Scaled Score Range	Raw Score	Expected Scaled Score Range	Raw Score	Expected Scaled Score Range
0	120–120	34	131–140	68	153–162
1	120–120	35	132–141	69	153–163
2	120–120	36	132–141	70	154–163
3	120–120	37	133–142	71	155–164
4	120–121	38	133–143	72	155–164
5	120–121	39	134–143	73	156–165
6	120–122	40	135–144	74	157–166
7	120–123	41	135–144	75	157–166
8	120–123	42	136–145	76	158–167
9	120–124	43	137–146	77	159–168
10	120–124	44	137–146	78	159–168
11	120–125	45	138–147	79	160–169
12	120–126	46	139–148	80	161–170
13	120–126	47	139–148	81	161–170
14	120–127	48	140–149	82	162–171
15	120–128	49	141–150	83	162–172
16	120–128	50	141–150	84	163–172
17	120–129	51	142–151	85	164–173
18	121–130	52	142–152	86	164–173
19	121–130	53	143–152	87	165–174
20	122–131	54	144–153	88	166–175
21	122–132	55	144–153	89	166–175
22	123–132	56	145–154	90	167–176
23	124–133	57	146–155	91	168–177
24	124–133	58	146–155	92	168–177
25	125–134	59	147–156	93	169–178
26	126–135	60	148–157	94	170–179
27	126–135	61	148–157	95	170–179
28	127–136	62	149–158	96	171–180
29	128–137	63	150–159	97	172–180
30	128–137	64	150–159	98	172–180
31	129–138	65	151–160	99	172–180
32	130–139	66	152–161	100	173–180
33	130–139	67	152–161	101	174–180

This chart approximates how your raw score translates into an actual final LSAT score.

(Percentile Rankings on next page)

SCALED SCORES AND PERCENTILE RANKINGS FOR THE LSAT

LSAT Score Distribution Table

(Percentile Ranking)

Scaled Score	Est. % Below for LSAT*	Scaled Score	Est. % Below for LSAT*
180	99.9	149	43.9
179	99.9	148	41.0
178	99.8	147	36.6
177	99.6	146	32.3
176	99.5	145	29.6
175	99.4	144	26.2
174	99.1	143	22.4
173	98.9	142	20.0
172	98.4	141	17.2
171	98.0	140	15.1
170	97.6	139	12.2
169	96.8	138	10.9
168	96.0	137	8.5
167	95.1	136	7.5
166	93.9	135	6.2
165	92.8	134	4.7
164	90.9	133	4.0
163	89.6	132	3.3
162	87.7	131	2.7
161	85.6	130	2.1
160	82.9	129	1.5
159	80.4	128	1.2
158	77.8	127	0.9
157	74.4	126	0.7
156	70.7	125	0.5
155	67.6	124	0.4
154	64.2	123	0.3
153	60.0	122	0.2
152	55.7	121	0.1
151	52.1	120	0.0
150	47.7		

*The entries in this column reflect the estimated percentages of candidates scoring below the score given. Score distribution may vary from administration to administration.

LSAT
Practice Test

Section 1 – Logical Reasoning
Section 2 – Analytical Reasoning
Section 3 – Reading Comprehension
Section 4 – Logical Reasoning
Section 5 – Writing Sample

(Answer sheets appear in the back of this book.)

TIME: 35 Minutes
      26 Questions

DIRECTIONS: The questions in this section are based on the reasoning contained in brief statements or passages. For some questions, more than one of the choices could conceivably answer the question. However, you are to choose the **best** answer; that is, the response that most accurately and completely answers the question. You should not make assumptions that are by common sense standards implausible, superfluous, or incompatible with the passage. After you have chosen the best answer, blacken the corresponding space on your answer sheet.

1. No one can be on the baseball team who does not buy his own glove. If Nathan is not on the baseball team, Peggy will not date him.

Which of the following can be deduced from the statements above?

(A)   If Nathan buys a glove, he will be on the baseball team.
(B)   If Nathan buys a glove, Peggy will date him.
(C)   If Nathan makes the team, Peggy will date him.
(D)   If Peggy dates Nathan, he bought a glove.
(E)   If Nathan buys a glove, he will date Peggy.

Questions 2–3 are based on the following passage:

On February 1, 1985, President Reagan stated to Congress:

"In order for arms control to have meaning and credibly contribute to national security and to global or regional stability, it is essential that all parties to agreements fully comply with them. Strict compliance with all provisions of arms control agreements is fundamental, and this administration will not accept anything less. To do so would undermine the arms control process and damage the chances for establishing a more constructive U.S.-Soviet relationship."

2. Which of the following statements is a reasonable inference which can be drawn from the above passage?

(A)   President Reagan had evidence that the Soviets were cheating on past arms control agreements.
(B)   Arms control agreements are necessary for national security.
(C)   Reagan considered Soviet compliance with past treaties a prerequisite for future negotiations.

(D)   Reagan was skeptical of the merits of arms control agreements.
(E)   Since the Soviet Union wants good relations with the U.S., it can be expected to comply with past treaties.

3. Which of the following is a premise of the president's statement?

(A)   The arms control process is the responsibility of Congress, as well as the president.
(B)   Arms control treaties with which each side complies can contribute to global stability.
(C)   The U.S. must adopt the most advanced technology for verifying Soviet compliance with arms control treaties.
(D)   The superpowers can never trust each other enough to have faith in arms control negotiations.
(E)   Arms control negotiations should be abandoned in favor of increased expenditures on defense.

4. The phrase "public interest" or "national interest" is often used by government officials to justify their actions. Presidents refer to the national interest when they take military action abroad or call upon U.S. citizens to make sacrifices in accepting reductions in favored domestic programs. Interest groups, too, claim that their goals are in accord with the public interest. Such a claim is often heard when a business group asks for high tariffs to reduce "unfair" competition from foreign countries, or when an environmental organization asks for greater government regulation to prevent air and water pollution, or when a teachers' organization asks for increased expenditures on educational programs.

> GO ON TO THE NEXT PAGE ⟶

Which of the following may be inferred from the above argument?

(A) We should ignore the claims of officials and interest groups that say they are acting in the public interest.
(B) Public officials and interest groups are very likely to act in the public interest.
(C) There is very little doubt about what constitutes the public interest.
(D) The "public interest" is the commonly accepted standard by which to judge the actions of participants in the political process.
(E) Self-interested behavior by individuals and groups is a natural part of the political process.

5. Becker and Edberg, tennis players who are of equal ability, are playing a five-set match. They have played two sets and Edberg has won both. Smith reasons that it is highly unlikely for one of two players of equal ability to win three sets in a row. He decides to bet $100 on Becker in set three.

Which of the following is the best formulation of the principle presupposed in Smith's reasoning?

(A) If X, Y, and Z are each improbable, then the joint occurrence of them all is improbable.
(B) If X and Y are each improbable, then the occurrence of X, Y, and Z together is equally improbable.
(C) If the joint occurrence of X, Y, and Z is improbable, then each of X, Y, and Z is improbable.
(D) If the joint occurrence of X, Y, and Z is improbable, then Z is improbable, given that X and Y have occurred.
(E) If the joint occurrence of X and Y is improbable, then the occurrence of an analogous event, Z, is also improbable.

6. In a dissent to the Supreme Court's 1989 decision concerning First Amendment protection for flag burning, Chief Justice Rehnquist wrote the following:

"Uncritical extension of constitutional protection to the burning of the flag risks the frustration of the very purpose for which organized governments are instituted. The Court decides that the American flag is just another symbol, about which not only must

opinions pro and con be tolerated, but for which the most minimal public respect may not be enjoined. The government may conscript men to fight and die for the flag, but the government may not _____."

Based on the information in the passage, which of the following statements best completes the last sentence?

(A) prohibit the burning of the banner under which they fight.
(B) give them the support necessary to win.
(C) place any limits on speech.
(D) protect them in fighting for the flag.
(E) tell civilians back home not to disrespect them.

7. A man notable for the intensity of his religious convictions, Augustine cannot be said to have cared much about politics for its own sake — or even politics for the sake of the good life. Politics for the sake of God? Yes, but Augustine would have thought the emphasis strange. He was not a primary political theorist, but rather a theologian so powerful that his view of man touched almost every subsequent Western political theorist. He was a spokesman for the Church in the moment when it irreversibly came to terms with the political.

The passage as a whole supports which of the following conclusions?

(A) If Augustine had not been a theologian, he would not have influenced the development of political theory.
(B) Since Augustine's writing was mainly theological, his influence on political theory was minimal.
(C) If Augustine had been a political theorist, his influence on theology would have been substantial.
(D) A discussion of Augustine's writings should not be included in a book on political theory.
(E) Augustine's view of man influenced the development of political theory.

GO ON TO THE NEXT PAGE

Questions 8–9 refer to the following passage:

The English constitution developed slowly over several hundred years and has never been formalized into one document. French constitutions — and there have been 17 of them since the Revolution — are always spelled out with logic and clarity. Whereas the Americans regard their constitution with an almost religious awe, not to be touched in its basic provisions, the French, and most European countries other than Britain, have seen constitutions come and go and are not averse to rewriting the basic rules of their political game every few decades.

8. Which of the following can be validly inferred from the facts or premises expressed in the passage above?

(A) The American constitution is outdated because of citizens' attitude toward it.

(B) The French value logic and clarity in their political institutions, while Americans value continuity.

(C) The Americans are more like the French than they are to the English in their attitudes toward constitutional change.

(D) Americans see their politics as a region.

(E) Most countries stick to one constitution and do not amend it.

9. Which of the following is the primary purpose of the passage?

(A) To contrast the French attitude toward constitutional change with that of the Americans and English.

(B) To show that constitutions may be changed often in developed countries.

(C) To show that comparative studies of the constitutions of other nations can be fruitful.

(D) To prove that the French constitution is better than the English or American constitutions.

(E) To introduce the reader to a discussion of the English constitution.

Questions 10–11 refer to the following passage:

It is clear that families, in some form, have always been found in human societies. Even in modern societies, with many opportunities for alternative life-styles, the family remains strong.

Much has been written about the high divorce rate in the United States, and some writers suggest the American family is on the verge of extinction. Nothing can be further from the truth. The high American divorce rate is accompanied by the highest rate of remarriage in the world.

10. Which of the following conclusions can be reasonably inferred from the above passage?

(A) The high divorce rate in the U.S. is a sign of the strength of the family.

(B) The American family is not becoming extinct, it is only changing.

(C) The high rate of remarriage in the U.S. is to be expected, given the high divorce rate.

(D) Modern views on the family are similar to ancient ones.

(E) Americans' views on family life are representative of the views of peoples in other nations.

11. According to the passage, which of the following is true?

(A) There are many benefits for a society served by a healthy family system.

(B) The family has actually become stronger with the development of modern society.

(C) At one point in social evolution the family was the master institution.

(D) The family is a basic institution of human society.

(E) Throughout history the family has been an important economic unit.

12. In the earliest human societies social control was the exclusive task of the kinship system. The dominant family member, often a dominant male, would enforce social control within the family. Or in more democratic kinship systems, social control was enforced collectively against deviant members. The kinship system also had the task of enforcing social control externally. If a family member was injured by someone from outside, other members of the family were responsible for avenging the wrong.

Which of the following objections, if true, would be logically relevant to the argument above?

GO ON TO THE NEXT PAGE ⟩

(A)	Studies have shown that in some ancient societies' families, females were dominant.
(B)	Ancient Sumerian tablets which have just been translated indicate that families put members to death for violating rules against incest.
(C)	Social scientists are, by and large, not interested in ancient methods of social control.
(D)	Deviant members are dealt with on a one-to-one basis.
(E)	Families let a jury decide the punishment for harming one of their own.

13.	There are students, as well as faculty, who are active in campus politics. All who are active in campus politics are encouraged to join the University Governing Board.

If the statements above are true, which of the following must also be true?

(A)	All who are encouraged to join the University Governing Board are active in campus politics.
(B)	All who are encouraged to join the University Governing Board are faculty or students.
(C)	Some who are encouraged to join the University Governing Board are not students or faculty.
(D)	Some students are encouraged to join the University Governing Board.
(E)	Some students are not encouraged to join the University Governing Board.

14.	I love you. Therefore, I am a lover. All the world loves a lover. Therefore, you love me.

In terms of its logical structure, the argument above most closely resembles which of the following?

(A)	Adam is a man. Men are homo sapiens. Therefore, Adam is a homo sapien. Homo sapiens are rational. Therefore, Adam is rational.
(B)	Sam got to work on time yesterday, the day before, and for the last 50 working days. Therefore, Sam is dependable. Dependable people get raises. Therefore, Sam will get a raise.

(C)	I like to talk to Pete. Therefore, I am a patient person. Everyone likes to talk to patient people. Therefore, Pete likes to talk to me.
(D)	An orderly universe had to be created by a rational God. The universe is orderly. Therefore, God is rational. A rational God would not allow sin to go unpunished. You sinned. Therefore, you will be punished.
(E)	Lifting weights strengthens the body. You lift weights, therefore, you are strong. Strong people are happy. Therefore, you are happy.

15.	If the college does not increase tuition, it must cut back expenditures for athletics. Cutting athletics will anger the alumni. If the alumni get angry, they may reduce donations. Reduced donations will result in decreased building maintenance. However, if the college raises tuition, the students will protest.

If all of the statements in the above are true, which one of the following statements must also be true?

(A)	Failure to increase tuition will result in decreased building maintenance.
(B)	Either the students will protest, or the alumni will be angry.
(C)	Reductions in donations will cause higher tuition.
(D)	Increasing tuition will result in greater funding for athletics.
(E)	There is no way for the college to continue the present levels of tuition and building maintenance.

16.	Voter registration drives have increased the percentage of the voting age population which is registered by 10% since 1950. However, the percentage of the voting age population which votes in presidential elections has declined by 15% since 1950. Therefore, the cause of the low turnout is not registration requirements, but the public's declining interest in national politics.

Which of the following statements, if true, would necessarily strengthen the conclusion above?

GO ON TO THE NEXT PAGE

(A) Voter turnout for state and local elections has also declined since 1950.

(B) Candidates for the presidency now campaign three weeks longer than they did in 1950.

(C) More people than ever view the government in Washington as too distant to help them solve their problems.

(D) People find it too difficult to register to vote.

(E) The voting age should be reduced.

17. Women's age at first marriage is directly related to their formal educational attainment. Moreover, early marriage influences later decisions by women on whether or not to further their formal education. Unfortunately, we cannot draw any conclusions from these observations because we know so little about the variables involved.

Which of the following is most probably the point to which the author's statements lead?

(A) Knowledge of the average age of first marriage for women is critical to understanding the educational needs of society.

(B) The relationship between marriage and educational attainment for women is worth studying.

(C) Early marriage discourages women from gaining further education.

(D) The relationship between marriage and education for women has been ignored by social scientists.

(E) Age at first marriage is the most important factor in predicting a woman's educational attainment.

Questions 18–19 refer to the following passage:

Truth is best discovered through dialogue. The lone individual, when presented with a problem, may reason his way to an answer. But the best test of that answer is its ability to overcome any plausible objections. It is for this reason that Plato presented his philosophy in the form of dialogues between Socrates and his fellow Athenians.

18. Following the logic in the above passage, if we believe that we have the correct answer to a question, but do not know what plausible objections to it may exist, we could believe it to be true for any of the following reasons EXCEPT

(A) we are inclined to think it is the best answer.

(B) we know that it is better than alternative answers.

(C) a majority of people think it is true.

(D) it fits our preconceptions of what is true.

(E) it appears to explain the facts as we know them.

19. If a scientist presented a paper describing a new theory of cold fusion at a conference, but refused to accept comments and criticism from the audience, the author of the above passage would most likely

(A) disagree, because cold fusion is not a very controversial subject.

(B) disagree, because raising objections will make the audience more interested in the paper.

(C) disagree, because the comments might raise objections to the theory which the scientist has overlooked.

(D) agree, because the paper describes a theory, not an explanation which has been widely accepted.

(E) agree, because a conference is not the appropriate setting for a dialogue.

20. The assertions that government should pass minimum wage laws to assure everyone a tolerable standard of living have been bolstered recently by the argument that many employers would take advantage of unskilled laborers if they could. Yet, even if that were true, it would not follow that government should pass minimum wage laws. Many unskilled workers are not worth the minimum wage, and are thus effectively shut out of the job market by such laws.

The argument which the author makes in the above passage is based on the assumption that

GO ON TO THE NEXT PAGE ⟶

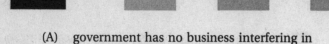

(A) government has no business interfering in employer-employee relations.
(B) employers will not hire employees who are not worth the minimum wage.
(C) employers, if left alone, would not take advantage of unskilled workers.
(D) government cannot effectively enforce minimum wage laws.
(E) unskilled workers should not look to government for economic aid.

21. The school newspaper's article yesterday concerning the health risks associated with eating foods cooked in animal fats had a positive impact. The cafeteria normally serves french fries cooked in animal fat, but today's menu had baked potatoes instead. One would assume the change was made because of yesterday's article.

A valid criticism of the above argument might emphasize that it

(A) draws an analogy between unrelated events.
(B) generalizes from one event to another event of the same kind.
(C) wrongly assumes that the cafeteria manager reads the school newspaper.
(D) questions the reasons for the cafeteria's switch from fried to baked potatoes.
(E) assumes that because one event occurs before another, the first event is the cause of the second.

22. The director of corporation R has been effective in streamlining the business, even though he has little previous experience with business management. Similarly, the director of corporation S has managed to increase profits, despite his lack of management training. Therefore, the fact that director of corporation T is new to business management will not necessarily have an adverse affect on his performance.

Which of the following assumptions underlies the above argument?

(A) Previous training and experience is undesirable for managers of corporations.

(B) What is true for the directors of some corporations may be true for directors of other corporations.
(C) Business management training is a prerequisite for a corporate director's success.
(D) Few corporate managers have previous business management training.
(E) Corporations do not seek to hire directors with previous training.

23. Despite the environmental damage caused by strip mining of coal, we must allow the project at Grand Bank to go ahead as scheduled. The National Energy Commission has estimated that demands for electrical power will increase by 12% in the tri-state region in the next 10 years. Besides, citizens of the three states have overwhelmingly expressed their opposition to building more nuclear power plants. Any surpluses of electrical power brought about by the Grand Bank Project can always be sold to other states in the region.

Which of the following, if true, would most seriously weaken the above argument?

(A) Past estimates of the National Energy Commission have underestimated future energy demands.
(B) Even with the Grand Bank project going full tilt, energy shortages might develop in the future.
(C) The state has reserves of natural gas which could fire electrical generators, and which have not been developed.
(D) Citizens have expressed no opinion on strip mining for coal.
(E) Coal-generated electricity is no cheaper than nuclear-generated electricity.

Questions 24–25 refer to the following passage:

Intelligent people always vacation in the Bahamas rather than in Hawaii. One can identify intelligent people by the fact that they have gone to the Bahamas rather than Hawaii.

GO ON TO THE NEXT PAGE

24. A logical criticism of the above argument would likely point out that the author

(A) uses the term "intelligent" in too broad a sense for it to have any meaning.
(B) generalizes from one example to prove a point about a whole class of people.
(C) presupposes the very point he is trying to establish.
(D) assumes that the Bahamas are a better vacation spot than Hawaii.
(E) fails to prove that the Bahamas are a better vacation spot than Hawaii.

25. The reasoning in which of the following passages is most like that in the passage above?

(A) Homemakers prefer Vizz to Cleansit for their household cleaning chores. Since homemakers are the best judges of home cleaning products, Vizz must be better.
(B) Homemakers prefer Vizz to Cleansit for their household cleaning chores. Vizz may be used on a variety of surfaces, therefore, it is the best choice.
(C) Advanced tennis players prefer the new oversized rackets to the standard sized ones. The oversized rackets have more power, which is why advanced players prefer them.
(D) People with class drive Porsches rather than Volkswagens. Porsches usually last longer than Volkswagens.
(E) People with class drive Porsches rather than Volkswagens. You can identify people with class by the fact that they drive Porsches.

26. Which of the following draws a conclusion about a group that is based upon a fact about its individual members?

(A) The office staff all go to Al's Grill for lunch. Therefore, we can find Lynn, the secretary, there at 12:00.
(B) I didn't like the looks of the red Camaro. When I buy one it will be blue.
(C) That chili tastes good. Therefore, the beans, peppers, and tomato sauce from which it is made also taste good.
(D) Each of the threads in the blouse is monochrome. Therefore, the blouse is monochrome.
(E) You can't trust Ed's advice on the stock market. He is a broker, and all they want to do is make a sale to get their commission.

STOP
If time still remains, you may review work only in this section. When the time allotted is up, you may go on to the next section.

TIME: 35 Minutes
23 Questions

DIRECTIONS: Each group of questions in this section is based on a set of conditions. In answering some of the questions, it may be useful to draw a rough diagram. Choose the response that most accurately and completely answers the question and blacken the corresponding space on your answer sheet.

Questions 1–5 refer to the following:

The class is going to perform the fairy scenes from *A Midsummer Night's Dream*. The roles to be performed are Oberon, Titania, Bottom, Puck, Peaseblossom and Cowslip.

From oldest to youngest, the performers are Allie, Bobby, Cary, Donny, Eddy, and Fergie, respectively.

The person playing Oberon is not Eddy, but is younger than the person playing Bottom.

The person playing Titania is younger than those playing Peaseblossom and Cowslip, but older than the one playing Puck.

The person playing Bottom is younger than the one playing Cowslip.

1. If the person playing Bottom is older than the one playing Peaseblossom, who must be playing Cowslip?

   (A) Allie   (D) Donny
   (B) Bobby   (E) Eddy
   (C) Cary

2. Which of the following is a possible arrangement of the players by role, from oldest to youngest?

   (A) Cowslip, Bottom, Oberon, Peaseblossom, Titania, Puck
   (B) Cowslip, Bottom, Oberon, Titania, Peaseblossom, Puck
   (C) Cowslip, Bottom, Peaseblossom, Titania, Oberon, Puck
   (D) Cowslip, Peaseblossom, Bottom, Puck, Titania, Oberon
   (E) Peaseblossom, Bottom, Cowslip, Oberon, Titania, Puck

3. If Cary plays Oberon, who must play Bottom?

   (A) Allie   (D) Eddy
   (B) Bobby   (E) Fergie
   (C) Donny

4. Which of the following CANNOT be a possible arrangement of players by role from oldest to youngest?

   (A) Cowslip, Peaseblossom, Bottom, Oberon, Titania, Puck
   (B) Peaseblossom, Cowslip, Bottom, Titania, Puck, Oberon
   (C) Cowslip, Peaseblossom, Puck, Bottom, Titania, Oberon
   (D) Peaseblossom, Cowslip, Bottom, Oberon, Titania, Puck
   (E) Cowslip, Peaseblossom, Titania, Puck, Bottom, Oberon

5. If Eddy plays Puck, which of the following must play Titania?

   (A) Bobby
   (B) Fergie
   (C) Donny
   (D) Allie
   (E) Bottom

Questions 6–11 refer to the following:

George, Henry, Irene, Janet, and Kay are members who would run for office if asked by the nominating committee, though none of them would run without such a request.

If George were asked to run, he would run.

If Henry were asked to run, he would run to prevent Kay from winning.

If Irene were invited to run, she would run just in case Janet did as well.

If Janet were asked, she would run just in case George did not.

If Kay is asked to run, she would run just in case Irene did not.

GO ON TO THE NEXT PAGE →

6. If all five were asked to run, how many candidates will run?

(A) 1   (D) 4
(B) 2   (E) 5
(C) 3

7. If all but George were asked to run, how many candidates will run?

(A) 0   (D) 3
(B) 1   (E) 4
(C) 2

8. If only Henry, Irene, and Kay are asked to run, which of them will run?

(A) Henry
(B) Irene
(C) Kay
(D) All of them will run.
(E) Henry and Kay will run.

9. If only George, Henry, and Irene are asked to run, which of them will run?

(A) George
(B) Henry
(C) Irene
(D) All of them will run.
(E) None of them will run.

10. Which of the following pairs of people could not run on the same slate?

(A) George and Henry
(B) George and Irene
(C) George and Kay
(D) Henry and Kay
(E) Irene and Janet

11. If the committee wanted both Henry and Janet to run, which of the following would they ask to run?

(A) George, Henry, and Janet only
(B) Henry, Irene, and Janet only
(C) Henry, Irene, and Kay only
(D) Henry, Janet, and Kay only
(E) Henry and Janet only

Questions 12–16 refer to the following:

The Weymouth Ferry was fully loaded except for space for six tons of deck cargo. The purser had ten crates that had not yet been brought aboard.

One crate weighed 1,000 pounds.

Two crates weighed a ton each.

Three crates each weighed a ton and a half.

The last four crates each weighed two tons.

12. What is the maximum number of these crates that can be stowed in the space available for deck cargo?

(A) 3   (D) 6
(B) 4   (E) 7
(C) 5

13. What is the minimum number of crates that can be taken aboard and exactly fill the available deck cargo space?

(A) 2   (D) 5
(B) 3   (E) 6
(C) 4

14. If the three ton-and-a-half crates are taken aboard, what is the maximum number of additional crates that can be stowed in the available space?

(A) 5   (D) 2
(B) 4   (E) 1
(C) 3

15. If the 1,000-pound crate costs $10 to ship, each one-ton crate costs $20, each ton-and-a-half crate costs $30 and each two-ton crate $25, what is the maximum shipping charge the purser can collect from the available tonnage?

(A) $75   (D) $120
(B) $90   (E) $150
(C) $110

GO ON TO THE NEXT PAGE

16. If the 1,000-pound crate cost $10 to ship, each one ton crate costs $20, each ton-and-a-half crate $30, and each two-ton crate $25, how much shipping charge is the purser guaranteed if he uses at least half the available tonnage?

(A) $40   (D) $55
(B) $45   (E) $60
(C) $50

Questions 17–21 refer to the following:

There are seven pieces left on the chessboard: the White King, White Queen, White Knight, White Rook, Black King, Black Bishop, and Black Pawn. From the point of view of the white player,

the White Rook, White King and Black Pawn are nearer than the White Queen, while the Black Bishop, Black King, and White Knight are farther away than the White Queen.

the White Rook is in the same column as the White Knight, but nearer.

the Black King is in the same column as the Black Pawn, but farther away.

twice as many pieces are to the right of the White Queen as are left of the White Queen.

the diagonal from the Black Pawn, going left and away from the White player, passes through the White Rook, White Queen, and Black Bishop, in order from near to far.

17. The White King lies in what direction from the White Queen?

(A) Toward the Black Player in the same column
(B) Away from the White Player in the same column
(C) Toward the White Player and to the left
(D) Toward the White Player and to the right
(E) Away from the White Player and to the right

18. What is the maximum number of pieces that might lie to the right of the Black King in the same row?

(A) 0   (D) 3
(B) 1   (E) 4
(C) 2

19. Which of the following statement must be true?

(A) The White Rook is nearer to the White Player than the Black Pawn.
(B) The Black Pawn is nearer to the White Player than the White King.
(C) The White King is to the right of the Black Bishop, from the White Player's point of view.
(D) The White Queen is to the right of the Black King, from the White Player's point of view.
(E) The White Knight is to the left of the Black King, from the White Player's point of view.

20. How many of the pieces may be nearer to the Black Player than the Black Bishop?

(A) 4   (D) 1
(B) 3   (E) 0
(C) 2

21. What is the maximum number of pieces that can be left of the White Rook, from the White Player's point of view?

(A) 0   (D) 3
(B) 1   (E) 4
(C) 2

Questions 22–23 refer to the following:

Breeders have discovered the following things about Connoisseur Cavies.

They come in three colors: Coal, Smoke, and Ash.

It is impossible to breed a pair of different colors successfully.

It is impossible to breed an offspring successfully with its parent.

Male offspring of a pair of Coals are Ash; female offspring of a pair of Coals are Smoke.

Female offspring of a pair of Smokes are Coal; male offspring of a pair of Smokes are Smoke.

Male offspring of a pair of Ashes are Coal; female offspring of a pair of Ashes are Ash.

GO ON TO THE NEXT PAGE

22. If a male cavy and his father are the same color, that color could

(A) only be Smoke.
(B) only be Coal.
(C) only be Ash.
(D) be any of the three except Coal.
(E) be any of the three colors.

23. If a female cavy is the same color as her granddaughter, which of the following must be true?

(A) They are both Coal.
(B) They are both Ash.
(C) The older is her granddaughter father's mother.
(D) The granddaughter is older's daughter's daughter.
(E) The granddaughter's mother is also the same color.

STOP
If time still remains, you may review work only in this section. When the time allotted is up, you may go on to the next section.

TIME: 35 Minutes
28 Questions

DIRECTIONS: Each passage in this section is followed by a group of questions to be answered on the basis of what is **stated** or **implied** in the passage. For some questions, more than one of the choices could conceivable answer the question. However, you are to choose the **best** answer; that is, the response that most accurately and completely answers the question, and blacken the corresponding space on your answer sheet.

Line

(1) The judicial branch is a coequal part of the United States government, and yet it has escaped the degree of scientific scrutiny given to the executive and legislative branches. This is not to say (5) the judicial branch has lacked all scrutiny, only that it has traditionally been viewed from a perspective different from the other two branches of government. The executive and legislative branches have traditionally been viewed as political entities. (10) Judges and the judicial branch have fostered the idea that they are nonpolitical arbiters of the law. In *Marbury v. Madison*, the landmark United States Supreme Court case which established judicial review under the United States Constitution, Chief (15) Justice John Marshall rhetorically asked who should determine the meaning of the Constitution. He answered himself by pointing to the fact that members of the other two branches were politically motivated, and only judges were qualified to be (20) truly nonpolitical arbiters of the law. These statements by Chief Justice Marshall were certainly not the beginning of what is generally known as the "cult of the robe," but they are a classic example in American jurisprudence.

(25) Following Marshall's reasoning, the study of the judiciary has traditionally used the case analysis method, which concentrates on individual cases. Each case must be decided on the basis of cases which have preceded it. Although it may be (30) acknowledged that each case differs from any other case in many ways, past cases must still be examined to find the general principles which are then applied to the present dispute.

This reliance on precedent, known in legal terms (35) as *stare decisis*, and its accompanying detailed examination of each case has caused legal scholars, to paraphrase Wieland, to not be able to see the forest for the trees. To get a more accurate picture of the workings of the judiciary it is necessary to (40) step back from the cases. One must remain cognizant of the details, but not to such a degree that they inhibit the ability to see the greater whole. This is not to say analysis of individual cases has no place in the scientific study of the judiciary. Indeed, (45) as was pointed out by Joyce Kilmer, there is always a place to appreciate the beauty of a tree, but there are also times when we must consider the tree as a part of the greater forest.

Although judicial scholars by and large do not (50) subscribe to the myth that judges are nonpolitical arbiters of the law, there is substantial interest in judicial biographies, and case studies. Judicial biographies and case studies are certainly useful in interpreting particular judicial decisions, (55) examining the opinions of a particular judge, or discussing specific points of law, but to optimize the results of such efforts, in terms of scientific study, such research must be viewed within the framework of a more comprehensive theory of (60) judicial decision making.

1. The primary purpose of the passage is to

(A) suggest that judges are political decision makers.
(B) complain that no one studies the judiciary.
(C) advocate another way of studying the judiciary.
(D) describe the case analysis method.
(E) attack the doctrine of judicial review.

2. Chief Justice Marshall's argument assumes

(A) judges are better educated than executives or legislators.
(B) politically motivated individuals are biased.
(C) only judges understand the Constitution.
(D) it is better to study individual cases.
(E) reliance on precedent is unnecessary.

3. According to the passage, the "cult of the robe" (line 23) can be best described as

(A) the interpretation of the Constitution.
(B) the study of prior cases.
(C) a method of studying the courts.

GO ON TO THE NEXT PAGE

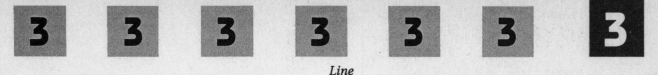

(D)   the use of individual cases in decision making.

(E)   the belief judges are neutral decision makers.

4. According to the author, the "cult of the robe"

(A)   should be studied more closely.

(B)   should be used instead of *stare decisis.*

(C)   has misled researchers.

(D)   has led to a lack of scientific study of courts.

(E)   has inhibited the study of individual cases.

5. The reference to Wieland in line 37 and 38 is intended to

(A)   advocate broader studies of the courts.

(B)   suggest that courts are organic entities.

(C)   argue that judges are political.

(D)   decry the use of precedent.

(E)   support the case analysis method.

6. The reference to Kilmer in lines 44–48 is intended to

(A)   point out the beauty of studying court.

(B)   argue that individual courts are un-important.

(C)   support reliance on precedent.

(D)   suggest case analysis has some benefits.

(E)   discourage belief in the "cult of the robe".

7. According to the author, the problem with detailed examination of each case is that

(A)   every case is different.

(B)   it does not recognize the political aspects of courts.

(C)   too many details obscure a broader understanding of how courts work.

(D)   it relies on the "cult of the robe".

(E)   one should ignore the details of cases.

8. The author's attitude toward case studies and judicial biographies can be summarized as being

(A)   skeptical   (D)   disdainful

(B)   supportive   (E)   indifferent

(C)   neutral

Line

(1)   Duke William the Conqueror's victory at Hastings guaranteed to him and his army a permanent stay in England. Harold, the one Anglo-Saxon leader of great ability, had perished and no

(5)   man or group of men left behind was equal to organizing successful resistance to the Normans. Thus, despite the fine opportunity that yet remained to inspire the mass of the Anglo-Saxons to heroic and stubborn resistance, there was no

(10) leadership to call it forth. It was now but a question of how long it would take the Normans to march around the island suppressing local and ill-organized defenses. Rightfully, some Anglo-Saxon lords and prelates regarded London as the key to

(15) defense and rallied the surviving forces there. They immediately elected as king Edgar the Etheling, the last male descendant of the West Saxon dynasty, to provide a symbol of resistance and unity. But he was a mere youth with no flair for leadership.

(20) Within five days of Hastings, William had his army on the march towards London. Dover and Canterbury fell without resistance, but he failed to take London Bridge by assault. Not having the equipment necessary to storm London, William fell

(25) to devastating a band of land encircling London, blocking all approaches. Deprived of reinforcements and obviously impressed by the terrible and methodical thoroughness with which William laid waste the approaches, some of Edgar's

(30) followers soon lost heart; the first to offer submission to William was Stigand, the Archbishop of Canterbury. The rest were soon to follow. A meeting was then held between William and the leading Anglo-Saxon lords and Londoners; the

(35) latter, realizing the futility of further fighting and the desirability of a strong ruler, agreed to cease resistance and surrender London. On Christmas Day William was crowned king of England in Westminster Abbey and was acknowledged lawful

(40) sovereign by the verbal assent of the assembled Anglo-Saxons and Normans. Meanwhile William strengthened his hold upon the new land, starting construction of castles such as the Tower of London, levying taxes to pay for his army, receiving

(45) the homage of lords, and confiscating the lands of those who had resisted his invasion. By March of 1067 he was so completely in control that he felt able to return to Normandy, leaving England under the direction of trusted Norman lieutenants.

GO ON TO THE NEXT PAGE →

(50) However much William's presence was required in his duchy, he had to neglect it for England within nine months. His lieutenants ruled a seething land too harshly and caused more discontent than order by their undiplomatic policies. The suppression of *(55)* an abortive attempt by Kentishmen to make the Norman Eustace of Boulogne king signaled to William the urgency for return. During the next eight years he was to be sporadically occupied in stamping out the last embers of Anglo-Saxon *(60)* resistance to foreign rule.

9. The primary purpose of the passage is to

(A) chronicle the exploits of William the Conqueror.
(B) describe the importance of London in the fall of England.
(C) show the importance of strong leadership.
(D) attack William's decision to return to Normandy.
(E) downplay the importance of Harold's death at Hastings.

10. According to the author, London was the key to England's defense but

(A) it could not withstand William's assault.
(B) it could not stand after being cut off.
(C) it fell due to the treachery of Anglo-Saxon lords.
(D) William conquered England without it.
(E) it did not resist William's advance.

11. Given the importance of a lack of leadership in England's fall, the author probably feels William's decision to return to Normandy to be

(A) unnecessary.
(B) important.
(C) of no consequence.
(D) ironic.
(E) administrative.

12. If William's lieutenants had ruled less harshly and more diplomatically William would not have been forced to return to England. According to the passage, this statement is

(A) unlikely, given the length of time William needed to stamp out resistance efforts.
(B) quite likely, given the necessity of administrative delegation.

(C) false since William did not leave England.
(D) irrelevant since William was from England. originally and would have returned anyway.
(E) unimportant since William would have returned to England in any event.

13. According to the author, the election of Edgar as king (lines 16-18) was to

(A) return a Saxon to the throne after Harold's defeat.
(B) serve as a rallying point for the remaining forces.
(C) prevent William from becoming king.
(D) follow the line of succession from Harold.
(E) abide by the English constitution.

14. According to the author, after Harold's death the fate of England was

(A) in serious doubt.
(B) dependent on the rise of another strong leader.
(C) in the hands of the archbishop of Canterbury.
(D) dependent on a counterattack from Normandy.
(E) clear as to the final result.

15. After his assault on London, William

(A) returned to Normandy.
(B) went to Hastings where he defeated Harold.
(C) marched to Kent to put down a rebellion.
(D) increased his power over England.
(E) defeated Edgar at Saxony.

Line
(1) The idea that moral rules are absolute, allowing no exceptions, is implausible in light of such cases as The Case of the Inquiring Murderer, and Kant's arguments for it are unsatisfactory. But are there *(5)* any convincing arguments against the idea, apart from its being implausible?

The principal argument against absolute moral rules has to do with the possibility of conflict cases. Suppose it is held to be absolutely wrong to *(10)* do A in any circumstances and also wrong to do B in any circumstances. Then what about the case in which a person is faced with the choice

GO ON TO THE NEXT PAGE

between doing A and doing B — when he must do something and there are no other alternatives
(15) available? This kind of conflict case seems to show that it is *logically* untenable to hold that moral rules are absolute.

Is there any way that this objection can be met? One way would be for the absolutist to deny that
(20) such cases ever actually occur. The British philosopher P. T. Geach takes just this view. Like Kant, Geach argues that moral rules are absolute; but his reasons are very different from Kant's. Geach holds that moral rules must be understood
(25) as absolute divine commands, and so he says simply that God will not allow conflict situations to arise. We can describe fictitious cases in which there is no way to avoid violating one of the absolute rules, but, he says, God will not permit
(30) such circumstances to exist in the real world.

Do such circumstances ever actually arise? The Case of the Inquiring Murderer is, of course, a fictitious example; but it is not difficult to find real-life examples that make the same point. During the
(35) Second World War, Dutch fishermen regularly smuggled Jewish refugees to England in their boats, and the following sort of thing sometimes happened. A Dutch boat, with refugees in the hold, would be stopped by a Nazi patrol boat. The Nazi
(40) captain would call out and ask the Dutch captain where he was bound, who was on board, and so forth. The fishermen would lie and be allowed to pass. Now it is clear that the fishermen had only two alternatives, to lie or to allow their passengers
(45) (and themselves) to be taken and shot.

Now suppose the two rules "It is wrong to lie" and "It is wrong to permit the murder of innocent people" are both taken to be absolute. The Dutch fishermen would have to do one of these things;
(50) therefore a moral view that absolutely prohibits both is incoherent. Of course this difficulty could be avoided if one held that only one of these rules is absolute; that would apparently be Kant's way out. But this dodge cannot work in every such case; so
(55) long as there are at least two "absolute rules," whatever they might be, the possibility will always exist that they might come into conflict. And that makes the view of those rules as absolute impossible to maintain.

16. The primary purpose of this passage is to

(A) discuss the role of Dutch fishermen during the Second World War.
(B) argue against absolute moral rules.
(C) show the difference between Kant and Geach.

(D) point out the inconsistency of moral rules.
(E) consider hypothetical philosophical problems.

17. According to the author, Geach's position (lines 20–30) is

(A) the Dutch fishermen were breaking the law so no conflict exists.
(B) absolute moral rules are an impossibility.
(C) the same as Kant's position.
(D) illustrated by The Case of the Inquiring Murderer.
(E) divine intervention prevents conflicts between absolute moral rules.

18. From the context of the passage, The Case of the Inquiring Murderer is most likely

(A) a hypothetical one, illustrating potential conflict.
(B) the name for the situation in which the Dutch fishermen found themselves.
(C) an example Geach used to illustrate his position.
(D) an argument in support of absolute moral rules.
(E) a real example of conflicting moral rules.

19. The author's attitude toward Kant's position is

(A) agreement.
(B) disbelief.
(C) indifference.
(D) reluctant acceptance.
(E) disdain.

20. According to the author, Geach finds cases of hypothetical conflict to be

(A) irrelevant to the real world.
(B) impossible to find.
(C) unlikely to occur.
(D) proof that absolute moral rules do not exist.
(E) an important support for Kant's position.

21. If there are at least two absolute moral rules the author argues

(A) they might not come into conflict.

GO ON TO THE NEXT PAGE

(B) only hypothetical cases will show potential conflict.
(C) the possibility of conflict detracts from the possibility of both being absolute.
(D) Geach's position is untenable.
(E) then one of them must not be absolute.

22. The author's basic argument is

(A) the impossibility of absolute moral rules.
(B) a denunciation of the writings of Kant.
(C) an illustration of the difference between free will and determinism.
(D) an example of the moral dilemma faced by the Dutch fishermen.
(E) a listing of important moral rules.

Line
(1)   The horseshoe crab (*Limulus*) was once thought to possess a primitive, simple eye that had been largely bypassed by evolution. In fact, evolution has served the crab well. Anatomical and physiological
(5) studies are showing that the 350-million-year-old animal has developed a complex, sophisticated visual system that incorporates elegant mechanisms for adapting its sensitivity to daily cycles of light and darkness.
(10)   Humans see only dimly at night, but the world of horseshoe crabs may be nearly as bright at night as during the day. Inquiry into the mechanisms by which *Limulus* performs this feat has added to knowledge of a most intriguing phenomenon. The
(15) brain and its sensory organs are not merely passive recipients of information from the outside world. Instead the brain actively controls those organs to optimize the information it receives.
        Over the past decade my colleagues and I have
(20) explored in considerable detail how horseshoe crabs adapt their visual systems. Our most important finding is the discovery of a 24-hour biological clock in the crab's brain that transmits nerve signals to its eyes at night. These signals work
(25) to increase the eyes' sensitivity to light by a factor of up to one million. Oddly enough, this extraordinary nighttime increase in sensitivity went undetected until the late 1970s even though the horseshoe crab's visual system is among the most thoroughly
(30) studied in the animal kingdom.
        The complex interaction between the brain and the eye of *Limulus* is only one example of the intricate relations between the brain and the sensory organs of almost all animals. The
(35) pioneering neuroanatomist Santiago Ramon y Cajal first uncovered two-way communication between the brain and the eye of a bird in 1889; he

found connections between neurons in the upper brain stem and neurons in the retina. In 1971
(40) Frederick A. Miles of the National Institutes of Health showed that these connections carry signals that change the way the retina codes spatial information and so should alter the way a bird sees its world.
(45)   Similar efferent connections have been found in many other animals, from the nerves that heighten overall sensory response in some fish to those that transmit signals from the brain to the ear in humans and other primates. Efferent neural
(50) connections from other parts of the brain outnumber the afferent connections from the optic nerve in the human lateral geniculate nucleus, where the initial stages of visual processing are performed. It appears that the
(55) brain, as much as the eye, determines how people see.
        People and birds are complicated, however; no one knows exactly how they see, much less how their brains modulate that vision. The work done
(60) on simpler neural systems such as *Limulus* may help elucidate such questions in more complicated species. Ultimately a series of ever more complex studies, founded on work on the horseshoe crab, may explain how the incomplete
(65) and unstable picture that sensory organs provide, modulated both by the brain and the environment, gives rise to such direct and incontrovertible impressions as the image of a sunset, the smell of a rose or the sound of a Bach
(70) fugue.

23. The primary purpose of the passage is to

(A) complain not enough research has been done on the horseshoe crab.
(B) suggest that the brain has some control over what the eye sees.
(C) point out the similarities between the visual systems of humans and crabs.
(D) describe the types of neural connections.
(E) argue that the visual systems of crabs are too simple to study.

24. The author has studied

(A) the nocturnal activities of horseshoe crabs.
(B) the reasons for human inability to see at night.

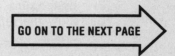
GO ON TO THE NEXT PAGE

(C) two-way communication between the eye and the brain.

(D) the primitive visual system of *Limulus*.

(E) adaptation in the visual system of *Limulus*.

25. The mention of the crab's "24-hour biological clock" in line 22 and 23 refers to

(A) the great age of this creature.

(B) the fact that the crab never sleeps.

(C) how nerve signals are attuned to regular changes in light levels.

(D) the reproductive cycle of *Limulus*.

(E) the activity cycle of horseshoe crabs compared to birds and humans.

26. According to the author, his most important finding involves

(A) the discovery that the crab's brain is an active part of its visual system.

(B) the discovery of the similarities between visual systems of birds and crabs.

(C) realization of how people see.

(D) the discovery that the human visual system is derived from that of the crab.

(E) a determination of the age of *Limulus*.

27. From the passage, efferent connections are most likely

(A) the stems which attach the crab's eye to its body

(B) a neural connection found exclusively in birds

(C) a kind of timer for the crab's biological clock

(D) connections which carry two-way communications

(E) what causes humans to see dimly at night

28. According to the author, the study of the visual system of horseshoe crabs

(A) may lead to greater understanding of more complex systems

(B) is of little importance

(C) explains why crabs have survived so long

STOP
If time still remains, you may review work only in this section. When the time allotted is up, you may go on to the next section.

TIME: 35 Minutes
      24 Questions

<u>DIRECTIONS</u>: The questions in this section are based on the reasoning contained in brief statements or passages. For some questions, more than one of the choices could conceivably answer the question. However, you are to choose the **best** answer; that is, the response that most accurately and completely answers the question. You should not make assumptions that are by common sense standards implausible, superfluous, or incompatible with the passage. After you have chosen the best answer, blacken the corresponding space on your answer sheet.

1. I had stuck to my resolution of not eating animal food. I considered the taking of every fish as unprovoked murder, since none of them could ever do us any injury that might justify the slaughter. But, I had formerly been a great lover of fish, and when one came out of the frying pan, it smelled appetizing. I balanced between principle and inclination, till I recollected that, when the fish were opened, I saw smaller fish taken out of their stomachs; then thought I, "If you eat one another, I don't see why we can't eat you."

Which sentence below best characterizes the writer's conclusion?

(A)   Fish eat other fish.
(B)   It is murder to eat fish.
(C)   There is nothing wrong with eating fish.
(D)   Fish smell appetizing in a frying pan.
(E)   We shouldn't eat animal food.

2. John, I know you're soft on this and I forgive you, but the fact is we own everything. They don't own their own backsides. We own them. We own them because we're better. There isn't anything that we can't own in any corner of the world wherever we might want it. (Name your tastes, John. These people are our servants....) Why shouldn't we enjoy ourselves?

From this passage which of the following may the reader conclude?

(A)   The speaker thinks he owns John.
(B)   The speaker regards John as an equal.
(C)   John is a servant of the speaker.
(D)   The speaker really does own everything.
(E)   John doesn't enjoy anything.

3. The spectacle of the dead whose bones were always being brought up to the surface of the cemeteries, as was the skull in *Hamlet*, made no more impression upon the living than did the idea of their own death. They were as familiar with the dead as they were familiar with the idea of their own deaths.

Which of the following is NOT support for the writer's conclusion?

(A)   The cemeteries' surfaces displayed bones.
(B)   The people discussed in the passage were impressed by death.
(C)   The death of others was familiar.
(D)   The death of oneself was expected.
(E)   There is a skull in *Hamlet*.

4. I want to discuss the view that the respect and tolerance due from one system to another forbids us to ever criticize any other culture. This "moral isolationism" is not forced upon us, and it makes no sense at all. People take it up because they think it is respectful. Nobody can respect what is entirely unintelligible to them. To respect someone, we have to know enough about him to make a *favorable* judgment, however general and tentative.

Which of the following is NOT a premise for the writer's conclusion?

(A)   We cannot respect what we do not find intelligible.
(B)   Respect implies a favorable judgment.
(C)   A favorable judgment implies some knowledge of the object of the judgment.
(D)   We should never criticize any other culture.
(E)   Moral isolationism is not respectful.

5. Never before had Boris Yeltsin gone so far as to demand that Mikhail Gorbachev relinquish his power. In the power struggle in the Soviet Union, Yeltsin has consummated the divorce between Gorbachev and the "reform camp" —

GO ON TO THE NEXT PAGE ➡

of which Yeltsin has become the nearly uncontested leader, thanks to Soviet leaders who have turned to the right. It would appear that the U.S.S.R. has entered a phase in which even the lowest of blows is permitted. By publicly demanding the resignation of the Soviet President, Yeltsin has crossed the line beyond any possible reconciliation with Gorbachev.

If the assertions in this passage are true, which assertion below must also be true?

(A)   Yeltsin is the Soviet President.
(B)   Yeltsin and Gorbachev may reconcile.
(C)   Yeltsin has not taken a turn to the right.
(D)   Gorbachev is a member of the reform camp.
(E)   Gorbachev is the uncontested leader of the U.S.S.R.

6. The exact risk of a patient contracting HIV from an infected surgeon is not known, but hospital officials say the risk is low. "No one has ever found a case in the medical field," says John Bartlett, director of the Hopkins AIDS program. Last year, a patient reported contracting AIDS from a dental surgeon, but the allegation has not been proven. As of December 1st, the Federal Centers for Disease Control reported 24 documented cases and 16 possible cases of health care workers contracting HIV through their jobs.

Which proposition below, if true, would strengthen the hospital officials' conclusion?

(A)   The allegation of the dentist's patient is false.
(B)   There were only 20 documented cases of health care workers contracting HIV.
(C)   There really were 16 possible cases of health care workers contracting HIV, in addition to the 24 documented cases.
(D)   The dentist mentioned had never been tested for HIV.
(E)   John Bartlett was a surgeon at Hopkins.

7. Scientific and technologic innovations produce changes in our traditional way of perceiving the world around us. We have only to think of the telescope, the microscope, and space travel to recall that heretofore unimagined perceptions of the macrocosm and the microcosm have

become commonplace. Yet, it is not only perceptions, but also conceptions of the familiar, that have become altered by advances in science and technology. If the mind is nothing but electrical processes occurring in the brain, how can we explain Einstein's ability to create the theory of relativity or Bach's ability to compose the Brandenburg Concertos?

Which of the following is most likely the writer's conclusion?

(A)   The microcosm and macrocosm have become commonplace.
(B)   There are heretofore unimagined perceptions.
(C)   The mind is nothing but electrical processes.
(D)   Advances in science and technology suggest that the mind is more than electrical processes.
(E)   The telescope, the microscope, and space travel are advances in science and technology.

8. *Today*'s biggest problem has been the defection of young female viewers. The show has made a number of major moves which have had two things in common: the problem with the young female audience has been made worse, and Gumbel has masterminded these moves. Not only has Gumbel helped exacerbate the alienation of female viewers, but he is also a problem himself. Although he is surely one of the most able broadcasters on television, Gumbel's Q score (the crucial measure of name-recognition and popularity with the American public) is now in the single digits.

Which of the following best summarizes the writer's argument?

(A)   Gumbel is in trouble because female viewers have alienated him.
(B)   Gumbel is one of the most able broadcasters on television, because his Q score is in the single digits.
(C)   Young female audiences are worse because the *Today* show is suffering.

GO ON TO THE NEXT PAGE

(D) Gumbel is a problem, because the *Today* show has made major moves.

(E) *Today* is suffering because Gumbel has alienated female viewers and his Q score is low.

9. Only the Eternal is always appropriate and present, and is always true. Only the Eternal applies to each human being, whatever his age. The changeable exists, and when its time has passed it is changed. Therefore, any statement about it is subject to change. That which may be wisdom when spoken by an old man about past events, may be folly in the mouth of a youth or of a grown man when spoken of the present. The youth would not be able to understand it and the grown man would not want to understand it.

If the propositions in this passage are true, which of the following must also be true?

(A) Any statement about the Eternal is subject to change.

(B) Wisdom about past events is not Eternal.

(C) The Eternal does not apply to youth or old men.

(D) Youth cannot understand wisdom.

(E) Grown men do not want to understand wisdom.

10. We assume that only by legal restraints are men to be kept from aggressing on their neighbors; and yet there are facts which should lead us to qualify our assumption. So-called debts of honor, for the nonpayment of which there is no legal penalty, are held more sacred than debts that can be legally enforced; and on the Stock Exchange, where only pencil memoranda in the notebooks of two brokers guarantee the sale and purchases of many thousands, contracts are safer than those which, in the outside world, are formally registered in signed and sealed parchments.

Which of the following propositions is NOT supported by this passage?

(A) Debts of honor cannot be enforced legally.

(B) We should qualify our assumptions that only by legal restraints are men to be kept from aggressing on their neighbors.

(C) Formally registered contracts are not necessarily safer than contracts made between two Stock Exchange brokers who note the contracts in their notebooks.

(D) Only by legal restraints are men to be kept from aggressing on their neighbors.

(E) Some nonlegally enforceable debts are more sacred than those that can be legally enforced.

11. It should be borne in mind that the knowledge which the men of A.D. 3000 will possess, if all goes well, may make all our aesthetics, all our psychology, all our modern theory of value, look pitiful. Poor indeed would be the prospect if this were not so. The thought, "What shall we do with the powers which we are so rapidly developing, and what will happen to us if we cannot learn to guide them in time?" already marks for many people the chief interest of existence.

Which of the following is NOT a premise of this passage's argument?

(A) Our aesthetics, psychology, and modern theory of value look pitiful.

(B) It would be bad if knowledge did not improve.

(C) Our powers are rapidly developing.

(D) We should be able to guide our rapidly developing powers in time.

(E) For many people rapid development of our powers is their chief interest of existence.

12. Analysis shows that magic rests everywhere on two fundamental principles: first, that like produces like, effect resembles cause; second, that things which have once been in contact continue ever afterwards to act on each other. The former principle may be called the Law of Similarity; the latter, that of Contact of Contagion. From the one, the magician infers that he can produce any effect he desires merely by imitating it in advance; from the other, it is inferred that whatever he does to a material object will automatically affect the person with whom it was once in contact.

Which of the following are premises of the magician's argument?

(A) Like produces like.

(B) He can produce any effect he desires.

GO ON TO THE NEXT PAGE

(C) Whatever he does to a material object will automatically affect the person with whom it was once in contact.

(D) Things which have been in contact continue ever afterwards to act on each other.

(E) Both A and D are premises.

13. The saddest thing about the editor's rant against multiculturalism in the special issue "Race on Campus" is how little of this "new orthodoxy" actually exists. Believe me, Aristotle, Augustine, Milton, Shakespeare, Cervantes, and Hegel are alive and well in the academy. In fact, the juicy attacks by the multiculturalists have probably gotten more students to read these books than any dry appeal to the "best that has been said or thought." There's nothing like a charge of intellectual obscenity to pack the house.

Based on this passage, which of the following is a position of the editor who ranted against multiculturalism?

(A) Little of the new orthodoxy of multi-culturalism exists.

(B) Aristotle, Augustine, and Milton are alive and well in the academy.

(C) A charge of intellectual obscenity will pack the house.

(D) Juicy attacks by the multiculturalists have gotten students to read books.

(E) There is a new orthodoxy of multi-culturalism.

14. Few writers have inspired more criticism, and more of it theoretically polarized and mutually hostile, than Ezra Pound. The critic who would engage Pound's work finds himself or herself framed from the outset by a kind of critical Cold War, one which forces him into something resembling the role of Marc Antony at the funeral in *Julius Caesar*. Pound critics come time and time again either to bury or to praise this strange and disturbing individual, who is seen by turns either as a fascist and anti-Semite in his very composition and genesis or as a literary genius.

Which of the following is NOT a premise of this passage?

(A) Pound was an anti-Semite.

(B) Pound is often seen as a literary genius.

(C) Pound is often seen as a fascist.

(D) Critics of Pound find themselves framed by a kind of critical Cold War.

(E) The critic often resembles the role of Marc Antony at the funeral in *Julius Caesar*.

15. Internships are historically common. References to apprenticeships are found as early as 2100 B.C. in the Code of Hammurabi. Greek and Roman sources also allude to this phenomenon. The concept was further developed in the English guilds of the Middle Ages, flourished through the 16th century in Europe, and even found its way to colonial America. Physicians' training includes a formal one-year internship after graduation. Similarly, the role an internship experience should play in legal assistant training programs and the value of an internship in meeting the needs of the student and the internship sponsor are extremely important today.

What is the main conclusion of this passage?

(A) Physicians' training includes a formal one-year internship after graduation.

(B) Internship programs are historically common.

(C) References to apprenticeships are found as early as 2100 B.C. in the Code of Hammurabi.

(D) Legal assistant trainees should have internships.

(E) Apprenticeships are similar to internships.

16. Textbooks have become the object of considerable attention in recent years and for good reason. Clearly, these packaged curricula are the essential source of information for students and teachers alike in public elementary schools. They outweigh all other sources in determining the day-to-day teaching and learning activities in classrooms. Their influence on the nature and consequences of elementary education is considerable, although not very well understood.

Which of the following is NOT one of the premises of this argument?

(A) Textbooks are packed curricula.

GO ON TO THE NEXT PAGE ▶

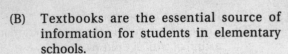

(B)   Textbooks are the essential source of information for students in elementary schools.

(C)   Textbooks are the essential source of information for teachers in elementary school.

(D)   Textbooks outweigh all other sources in determining the day-to-day teaching in classrooms.

(E)   Textbooks deserve the considerable attention they have been receiving.

17. Previous analyses of verbal content have shown that the three network television newscasts are much more alike than different in their story selection, story order, and portrayal of events on the evening news. Yet, there is no evidence to suggest that there is a corresponding similarity in visual form, or the state, structure, or character in which visual information or content appears. The visual form is important in conveying the meaning, significance, or aesthetic value of the visual content.

Which of the following, if true, would weaken this passage's argument?

(A)   Visual form is less important than verbal content.

(B)   Visual form conveys aesthetic value of visual content.

(C)   Network news stories and their verbal forms have remained static over the past 30 years.

(D)   The three networks tend to select similar stories.

(E)   There has been as much analysis of visual form as of verbal content.

18. The production of new translations of the Bible is an awesome task. One cannot even begin to calculate the thousands of hours of individual and committee work involved, without standing back in amazed appreciation for those who have committed themselves to such an undertaking. When we multiply the amount of labor expended on one such translation by the number of new translations that have exploded around us in recent years, it is clear that the modern world's hunger for the "Word" is no less than that of less media-saturated generations of long ago.

What is the conclusion of this argument?

(A)   There has been an explosion of translations of the Bible in recent years.

(B)   The production of new translations of the Bible is an awesome task.

(C)   The less media-saturated generations of long ago had a greater hunger for the "Word" than the modern world has.

(D)   We should multiply the amount of labor over one translation by the number of new translations.

(E)   People are as interested in the Bible today as they were before.

19. It looks as though I'll have to put new siding on the house this year. Dave next door just had to have his house done, and his place was built the same time as mine and by the same contractor.

Which of the following, if true, would most weaken the above argument?

(A)   The contractor guaranteed that the present siding would last for two more years.

(B)   The neighbor's siding is composition while the speaker's siding is redwood.

(C)   The speaker cannot afford new siding this year.

(D)   Dave, the neighbor, is an expert carpenter, but the speaker is not.

(E)   Dave and the speaker both wash their sidings annually.

20. The whole universe must have had a beginning, since each thing in it had a beginning.

Which is the principle fault in the above reasoning?

(A)   The speaker argues from the fact that each thing began at some time, to the claim that there was some one time at which all things began.

(B)   The speaker fails to take into account the question of what could have caused the universe to begin.

(C)   The speaker argues that the whole has some property simply because all of its parts do.

GO ON TO THE NEXT PAGE

(D) The speaker argues that one thing is similar to another in one property just because they are both similar in another property.

(E) The speaker fails to deal with the fact that things last for longer or shorter times and that the universe may, thus, be the longest-lasting thing.

21. When a mother says "Wise drivers buckle up" to her 16-year-old daughter who is about to take her first solo drive, she means "Buckle your seat belt." If she did not mean this, her remark would not be relevant to the daughter's situation, for, at that moment, the daughter has no interest in the apparent information her mother's remark seems to convey.

The speaker obviously assumes that

(A) teenagers are never interested in what wise drivers do.

(B) what is relevant to a person's situation rarely interests that person.

(C) the mother is worried about her daughter's safety.

(D) the meaning of a remark will be relevant to the hearer's situation.

(E) teenagers tend not to use seat belts when driving.

22. A recent study found that body builders who took steroids had significantly lower levels of high-density lipoproteins in their blood than did otherwise similar men who did not take steroids. The average was 50% lower for the steroid users, and the drop varied directly with the size of the steroid dose. Low levels of high-density lipoproteins in the blood are known to be correlated to high risk of heart attack.

Which of the following is the most accurate conclusion of the study discussed?

(A) Body building is hazardous to the builder's health.

(B) Taking steroids causes heart attacks.

(C) Taking steroids significantly increases the likelihood of a heart attack.

(D) Taking steroids lowers the level of high-density lipoproteins in the blood.

(E) Body building lowers the level of high-density lipoproteins in the blood.

23. The fact that a person is an expert in one field does not give his statements about other areas any special force. So, when Dr. Spock, the famous baby doctor, talks about problems in the world economy, we should

(A) reject what he says, since this is not his field.

(B) accept his views, since he is an expert.

(C) subject his views to the same scrutiny we would give anyone else's.

(D) ignore his views, since he is only a baby doctor.

(E) accept his view if he is found to be an expert on the world economy as well.

24. If Einstein's theory is correct, then light from certain stars, which are actually behind the sun, can be seen during a total solar eclipse. The standard theory holds that this light cannot be seen, since the sun is in the way. But, at every eclipse since Einstein's theory was published, such stars have been seen and photographed. Thus, Einstein's theory is clearly true.

This case is most like which of the following in its logical features?

(A) Copernicus explained the known phenomena with an explanation that contradicted the standard theory.

(B) Kepler explained some recently discovered, and not yet explained phenomena, with an explanation that contradicted the standard theory.

(C) Galileo observed moons around Jupiter, where the standard theory said moons could not exist.

(D) Halley correctly predicted the appearance of a comet, which the standard theory said could not be done, on the basis of a new theory.

(E) Herschel discovered Uranus by looking exactly where the standard theory said a new planet should be.

STOP
If time still remains, you may review work only in this section. When the time allotted is up, you may go on to the next section.

DIRECTIONS: You have 30 minutes in which to plan and write the brief writing exercise on the topic below. Read the topic carefully. You will probably find it best to spend a few minutes considering the topic and organizing your thoughts before you begin writing. **Do not write on a topic other than the one specified. Writing on a topic of your own choice is not acceptable.**

There is no "right" or "wrong" position on this topic. Law schools are interested in how skillfully you support the position you take and how clearly you express that position. How well you write is much more important than how much you write. No special knowledge is required or expected. Law schools are interested in organization, vocabulary, and writing mechanics. They understand the short time available to you and the pressure under which you are writing.

Confine your writing to the lined area inside the booklet. Only the blocked lined area will be reproduced for the law schools. You will find that you have enough space if you plan your writing carefully, write on every line, avoid wide margins, and keep your handwriting a reasonable size. Be sure that your handwriting is legible.

The writing sample is photocopied and sent to law schools to which you direct your LSAT score. Use only the pen provided at the test center to complete the writing sample; this will ensure a photocopy of high quality. (Pens are *not* used on the computerized answer sheet; this requires a No. 2 pencil.)

SAMPLE TOPIC

Baldwin State University is located in Los Angeles, California and is required to accept California high school students who graduate in the top 20 percent of their class. The university is striving to enhance its image as a progressive, quality school. It is also trying to recruit top-notch faculty members. Two candidates are finalists for a tenure-track position in the Mathematics Department of Baldwin State with a specialization in statistics. You, as a faculty member, must write a recommendation supporting the appointment of one of the finalists. Baldwin State's guidelines for the appointment indicate that the university:

- is looking for an assistant professor who is both a teacher and a scholar

- considers teaching, research, and university service (in that order), the criteria for promotion and tenure.

The first finalist is Ms. Margaret Jones, 26, who has just completed her doctorate in statistics from Yale University and graduated with highest honors. Jones received her B.A. degree from Oberlin College and her M.A. degree from the University of Pennsylvania, both degrees are in mathematics. She already has one year of full-time teaching experience in addition to three years as a Teaching Assistant. Her reviews from students are mixed and on a scale of 1 to 5 (with 5 being the highest), she averages a 2.85 on the question, "Rate the effectiveness of this instructor." Although she is friendly, Jones has a nervous personality, talks rapidly, and tends to give answers which are longer than necessary when questioned. She holds regular office hours, but is generally unwilling to meet with students beyond those hours. Jones has co-authored three textbooks on mathematics and is currently working on her own book about statistics. She has assured the Mathematics Department of Baldwin State that she is eager to pursue her research agenda at the university.

Mr. John Smith is the other finalist. Smith is 30 years old and holds a doctorate in statistics from Oregon State University and a B.A. degree from Iowa State University where he majored in philosophy and economics. His M.A. degree was from the University of Washington-Seattle, where he majored in mathematics and took a minor in economics. Smith has three years of full-time teaching experience at the University of West Virginia and several years experience as a part-time lecturer and teaching assistant. His evaluations from students are exceptionally positive and they especially note his patience and willingness to spend extra time with them. His relaxed personality also encourages student participation in the classroom. Smith has thus far published two papers in respected journals and is co-authoring a textbook on statistics with applications to various fields. His research background is somewhat weak, but meets all university requirements.

STOP

If time still remains, you may review work only in this section.

LSAT PRACTICE TEST
ANSWER KEY

Section 1 – Logical Reasoning	
1. (D)	14. (C)
2. (C)	15. (B)
3. (B)	16. (C)
4. (D)	17. (B)
5. (D)	18. (B)
6. (A)	19. (C)
7. (E)	20. (B)
8. (B)	21. (E)
9. (A)	22. (B)
10. (B)	23. (C)
11. (D)	24. (C)
12. (B)	25. (E)
13. (D)	26. (D)

Section 2 – Analytical Reasoning	
1. (A)	13. (B)
2. (A)	14. (D)
3. (B)	15. (D)
4. (C)	16. (B)
5. (C)	17. (C)
6. (C)	18. (A)
7. (C)	19. (E)
8. (E)	20. (C)
9. (A)	21. (D)
10. (B)	22. (A)
11. (D)	23. (D)
12. (C)	

Section 3 – Reading Comprehension	
1. (C)	15. (D)
2. (B)	16. (B)
3. (E)	17. (E)
4. (D)	18. (A)
5. (A)	19. (B)
6. (D)	20. (A)
7. (C)	21. (C)
8. (A)	22. (A)
9. (C)	23. (B)
10. (B)	24. (E)
11. (D)	25. (C)
12. (A)	26. (A)
13. (B)	27. (D)
14. (E)	28. (A)

Section 4 – Logical Reasoning	
1. (C)	13. (E)
2. (B)	14. (A)
3. (B)	15. (D)
4. (D)	16. (E)
5. (C)	17. (A)
6. (A)	18. (E)
7. (D)	19. (B)
8. (E)	20. (C)
9. (B)	21. (D)
10. (D)	22. (D)
11. (A)	23. (C)
12. (E)	24. (D)

Detailed Explanations of Answers

Section 1 –
Logical Reasoning

1. **(D)** Answer (A) assumes that buying a glove is the only requirement for being on the team. There may be other, unstated, requirements, such as a tryout, or age restrictions. A premise may state "if not A, then not B." A reader may not assume on that basis "if A, then B." That is an invalid assumption. Answer (B) makes the same error as Answer (A), but makes it twice. Just because he buys a glove does not mean he will make the team. In addition, that he makes the team does not mean Peggy will date him. We know that if he does not make the team, she will not date him. This does not mean that if he does, she will. Answer (C) repeats the second mistake of Answer (A). In Answer (D) Peggy dates Nathan. We know that making the team was necessary for that. We also know that buying the glove was necessary for making the team. Therefore, he bought the glove. Answer (E) assumes that if he buys the glove he will make the team. (See explanation for (A).) It also assumes that if he makes the team, he will want to date Peggy, and that she will date him. None of this is established.

2. **(C)** Answer (A) need not be true. Reagan might have merely suspected Soviet non-compliance. Or he may have made the statement to ward off anticipated non-compliance. This answer asks you to assign a motive for the President's statement, when many different motives are possible. Answer (B) is not supported by the statement. Reagan says that compliance is necessary in order for arms control agreements to contribute to security. This implies that arms control negotiations with which one side does not comply might actually damage the other side's security. Answer (C) is supported by the following: Reagan says that his administration would not accept anything but full compliance with (present) treaties. Acceptance of non-compliance would undermine the arms control process and damage the U.S.-Soviet relationship. An undermined negotiation process and a damaged relationship suggest no more negotiations. Answer (D) cannot be right, since Reagan implies in the first sentence that arms control treaties with which each side complies can contribute to security. Answer (E) is not correct, because the passage gives no information about Soviet desires or intentions. Even if the Soviets want good relations, one could not rule out the possibility that they might cheat if they thought no one would find out.

---

3. **(B)** Answer (A) gains little support from the passage. The president's statement is made to Congress, but Congress is not asked to cooperate with the president, or to do anything else. Answer (B) is supported by sentence one. The sentence states that in order for arms control to have meaning and credibility both sides must comply. This, of course, implies that arms control agreements with which both sides comply can increase global stability. Answer (C) is a possible conclusion which one could draw from the statement. It is not a premise of it. Nor is it supported by the statement. Reagan has identified a desired outcome, compliance with treaties, but has not hinted at how that outcome might be achieved. Answer (D) assumes that the two sides' faith in the treaty depends only on trust. It might depend on other factors, such as the technology available — or the methods adopted in a treaty — for verifying compliance. Answer (E) is without support for two reasons: 1. Reagan does not imply that arms control should be abandoned, only that compliance should be required; 2. he says nothing about preferring measures other than arms control for promoting national security.

---

4. **(D)** (A) While officials and groups often make this claim, they are not always being truthful. However, they may sometimes be. Instead of merely ignoring the claim, we must judge its truthfulness. (B) Even though they often claim to be, there is no reason, based on the passage, that they are making truthful claims. (C) If there was little doubt, then specious claims would present no problem. We would know immediately if a claim was false, and the group or official could easily be held responsible by the public for lying. (D) Since officials and groups attempt to justify their behavior by saying it furthers the public interest, they must be assuming that that is the standard by which the public will judge them. (E) While this may be true, it is not substantiated by the passage. The passage says nothing about whether self-interested or public interested behavior is more common or natural to the political process.

---

5. **(D)** The answer cannot be (A). X equals Edberg winning set 1; Y equals Edberg winning set 2; and Z equals Edberg winning set 3. Any of these, taken alone, is equally probable or improbable, given that the players are of equal ability. Answer (A) assumes that each, taken alone, is improbable. Answer (B) is not correct, for the same reason. The answer assumes that X and Y are improbable, when they are, taken alone, equally probable or improbable. Answer (C) assumes that because it is improbable that Edberg will win three sets in a row, it is improbable that he win any of the first three sets. That is not what Smith assumes. What Smith does assume is that since Becker has a 50/50 chance of winning a given set, it is not likely that Becker will lose three in a row. Answer (D) is correct. Smith assumes that since Becker has a 50/50 chance of winning any given set, it is not likely that he will lose three in a row. Since he has lost two in a row, he is likely to win set three. Answer (E) is wrong because the statement says Smith assumes that it is unlikely one of two players of equal ability will win three sets in a row. It did not say he assumes that the player will not win two sets in a row. That is the assumption upon which the answer is based.

6. **(A)** This answer best completes the thought of the sentence. The passage states that the government may not prevent burning of the flag, which is the banner under which conscripted Americans fight. (B) Preventing flag burning is not the only way in which the government may support American soldiers. Nothing prevents the government from giving them support in the form of training and equipment, for example. (C) One cannot assume on the basis of the passage that government can place no limits on speech, only that it cannot prevent flag burning. (D) The passage does not say that the government cannot protect the men, either by supplying the best equipment or leaders. It only states that the government cannot stop flag burning. (E) Flag burnings might not be meant to show disrespect for fighting men. It might be a statement against an act of government which was unrelated to the draft or war.

---

7. **(E)** (A) While this may be true, it also may not. If Augustine had not become a theologian, he might have become a political theorist. In that capacity he might have influenced the development of political theory as much or more than he did. (B) The passage clearly states that Augustine's influence on political theory was great, since his view of man touched nearly almost every subsequent Western political theorist. (C) Just because he, being a theologian, influenced political theory, does not mean that had he been a political theorist he would have influenced theology. The passage does not establish that the influence of theology on political theory is reciprocal. (D) Since Augustine's influence on theory was substantial, one must understand his thought to know how it affected the subsequent development of political theory. Therefore, it is appropriate that a discussion of his work be included in a book on political theory. (E) This is clearly established by the passage, which states that his views touched almost every subsequent Western political theorist.

8. **(B)**   (A) This may not be inferred from the passage. Americans do not think that the basic provisions of their Constitution should be changed. However, it is entirely possible that those basic provisions are as timely now as when the Constitution was written. The passage does not indicate otherwise. (B) This is clearly inferred from the passage. French constitutions are always spelled out with logic; therefore, the French must value logic in their constitutions. Americans are unwilling to change the basic features of their Constitution; therefore, they must value continuity in their political institutions. (C) In the third sentence, the Americans and the British are portrayed as unlike the French and other Europeans. The way in which they are unlike the others is that they do not change their constitutions very often. Therefore, the Americans are more like the British than the French in their attitudes toward constitutional change. (D) The paragraph states Americans regard their Constitution with religious awe, not that they see it as a religion. (E) In the last sentence, it is stated that many countries rewrite the basic rules of their political game.

---

9. **(A)**   This is the best answer, because the passage shows that the British and Americans are averse to constitutional change, while the French are not. (B) The example cites examples of countries with as well as without constitutional change as well as the opposite. It never mentions the term "developed countries," as it should if the purpose was answer (B). (C) While this answer is plausible, it is not the best. The passage never refers to the advantages to be gained from such a study. Rather, it assumes as a given that such studies are fruitful. (D) The author never passes judgment on whether logic or continuity is preferable in a constitution. Therefore, this answer is not the best. (E). The primary emphasis in the passage is on the French, not the British constitution. First the French is compared to the British; next it is compared to the American.

10. **(B)** (A) The author says that the high divorce rate is interpreted by some as a sign of the weakness of the American family. He argues, however, that the high rate of remarriage offsets the high divorce rate. He is certainly not arguing that the high divorce rate, in itself, is a sign of the strength of the family. (B) This is the best answer. The high divorce rate and the high rate of remarriage are both changes which the family is currently experiencing in America. It is not, however, on the verge of extinction. As he says, nothing could be further from the truth than that the American family is becoming extinct. (C) If the high rate of remarriage could be expected, given the high divorce rate, the author would not need to supply this bit of information. As it is, he is compelled to supply the information in order to counter the argument that the high divorce rate shows a decline in the strength of the American family. (D) Nothing in the passage leads to such an inference. On the contrary, high divorce rates are said by the author to be cited by some as evidence of a decline in the family. Therefore, high divorce rates must mark a change in attitude toward the family. (E) The passage does not support such an inference. Rather, Americans' attitudes toward divorce seem to be different from those of other modern peoples, as evidenced by Americans' higher divorce rates.

11. **(D)** (A) The passage says nothing about the value of a healthy family system to society. (B) The passage is arguing that the family has not become weaker, not that it has gotten stronger. (C) One cannot deduce this on the basis of the passage. Perhaps it always was, and still is, the master institution. Perhaps it never was. One cannot tell, because of insufficient evidence. (D) This is the best answer. Since the family has always existed in human society, one may say that it is a basic institution of that society. (E) The passage says nothing about the economic aspect or function of the family.

12. **(B)** (B) is relevant. It substantiates the point of the passage, which is that kinship units practiced social control. (A) is not relevant. The passage states that the dominant member was often a male, which is the same as admitting that males were not always dominant. (C) is not relevant. The passage is concerned with making a point, not with what groups might be interested in the topic. (D) is not relevant to the argument because the passage states that deviant members were often dealt with collectively. (E) is also not relevant because it is stated in the last sentence that family members were responsible for avenging the wrong.

---

13. **(D)** (A) need not be true. That all who are active in campus politics are encouraged to join does not mean that everyone who is encouraged to join is active in campus politics. Some may not be active, yet be encouraged to join. Answer (B) need not be true. The passage states that all faculty and students who are active in campus politics are encouraged to join. This does not necessarily mean that others, who are not students or faculty, are not encouraged to join. Perhaps administrators or community leaders are also encouraged to join. Answer (C) need not be true. It is possible that only faculty and students are encouraged to join, and no one else. The passage does not specify. Answer (D) must be true. The passage states that there are students active in campus politics, and that all those in that category are encouraged to join. Answer (E) need not be true. It is possible that all students are active in campus politics. Therefore, all students would be encouraged to join.

---

14. **(C)** The argument is structured to show that certain feelings which one person has for another must be reciprocated. In other words, the feelings in the first person must produce like feelings in the second person. Answer (C) best parallels that type of reasoning. Only one difference occurs between the passage and Answer (C). In the passage, the object of the feelings is being addressed. In answering the object of the feeling was being spoken of in the third person. Answers (A), (D), and (E) employ standard syllogistic reasoning. The syllogism is the method used in deductive reasoning. The syllogism takes the form:

If $A = B$
And $B = C$
Then $A = C$

In Answer (A) the argument is:

Adam = Man
Man = Rational
therefore Adam = Rational

Answer (D) uses a slightly different formulation:

If A then B
A, so B
If B, then C cannot be present without D
B with C, therefore D follows

In the passage,

A = orderly universe
B = rational God
C = sin

---

15.   **(B)**   (A) This cannot be the answer. The alumni may or may not reduce donations if they get angry. If they do not reduce donations, maintenance may well stay the same. (B) The students will protest if tuition is raised. If tuition is not raised, athletics will be cut. This will anger alumni. So, either the students will protest, or alumni will be angry. (C) The statements do not establish a causal relationship between reductions in donations and higher tuition. The statements establish that reduced donations will cause less maintenance, and nothing else. The alumni may get angry about something other than cuts in athletics. Then they may reduce donations even though tuition is not increased. (D) Funding for athletics may remain constant even though tuition is increased. (E) The statements do not establish that alumni will get angry if athletics is cut, only that they may. Therefore, it is possible for tuition to be increased, for alumni not to get angry, and for donations and maintenance to remain the same.

---

16.   **(C)**   (C) If more people view the government in Washington as remote and of little help, this would strengthen the conclusion that their interest would be directed away from national politics. (A) The fact that turnout for state and local elections has declined might mean that interest in state and local politics has declined. This does not necessarily mean that interest in national politics has also declined. (B) Candidates may campaign longer for any number of reasons which are unrelated to declining interest in national politics. Perhaps there are more candidates, and the public needs longer to weigh their qualifications against each other. Perhaps the laws governing campaign financing have changed, and candidates now have more money to spend campaigning. (D) If this were true, it would not strengthen the conclusion but take away from it. (E) would not strengthen the conclusion nor take away from it.

---

17.   **(B)**   (A) This answer draws a conclusion from the statements, when the author says plainly that not enough is known about the variables to draw any conclusion. (B) The author establishes a relationship between age at first marriage and formal educational attainment and between early marriage and later decisions about getting more education. However, the variables are not understood. The author obviously thinks the relationship between marriage and educational attainment is worth studying, or he would not discuss the topic. Therefore, we may assume that he would like to see more work done in order to bring further information about the topic to light. (C) The author says that early marriage influences women's decisions about furthering their formal education. He does not say whether that influence is positive or negative. Answer (C) assumes the influence is negative. (D) We cannot assume that simply because all the variables are not understood, social scientists have ignored the topic. This cannot be true, according to the information given, because enough is known to establish the relationships which are discussed. This means that the topic has received some attention. (E) This is a conclusion. However, the author says that no conclusions can be drawn, since not enough is known about the variables. Perhaps the most important factor for predicting educational attainment is socio-economic background prior to marriage. We simply cannot tell, based on the passage.

---

18.   **(B)**   Choices (A), (C), (D), and (E) are possible choices. The only choice which is not possible is (B). According to the passage, the best test of an answer is its ability to overcome objections. If we do not know what objections to an answer exist, we have not seen the answer put to the test. If we have not seen it put to the test, we do not know how strong it is. Therefore, we cannot judge its strength relative to other possible answers.

---

19.   **(C)**   (A) One cannot judge, based on the passage, whether cold fusion is controversial or not. Even if it is not controversial, the author of the passage would argue that since the theory the scientist is presenting is new, he should accept criticism in an attempt to discover how well it meets plausible objections. (B) While this might be true, it would be of much less importance to the author of the passage than discovering the strength of the new theory. That could be done only by the scientist's accepting criticism and objections to the paper. (C) This is the best answer. By accepting comments, the scientist might discover objections to his new theory which he had previously overlooked. This would give him the opportunity to see if the theory could overcome the objections, or have to be modified in some way to accommodate those objections. (D) A theory is a tentative explanation of some phenomenon, which is deserving of consideration until it is proven wrong. For the scientist not to accept objections would mean that he was unwilling to have the theory tested to see if it was valid. Therefore, the author could not agree with the scientist's decision for the reason which answer (D) proposes. (E) A conference of scientists would be the perfect place for a dialogue about the merits of a scientific theory. Since both those presenting papers and those listening to presentations are likely to be well trained in the field, a very good dialogue could be expected.

20.   (B)   (A) The argument does not assume this. It does not argue, for example, that government should not pass laws to regulate overtime pay, or to maintain minimum working conditions. (B) This is the correct answer. The last sentence says that minimum wage laws shut out of the job market employees who are not worth that pay. To be shut out of the job market means not to be hired. The clear assumption is that employers do not hire such people. (C) The author leaves this question to the side in the sentence which reads "Yet, even if that were true...." Thus, the author is willing to grant the assumption that employers would sometimes take advantage of unskilled workers. (D) This cannot be the answer. If government could not enforce minimum wage laws, the laws would have no effect on the job market. The laws would not shut anyone out of the job market. (E) Again, the argument does not establish that government has no role to play in helping unskilled workers. Perhaps it should be responsible for unemployment benefits, national health care, or countless other such programs.

21.   (E)   (A) First, the statements do not draw an analogy. An analogy shows how one thing resembles another. The article and the menu change are not necessarily analogous. We do not know the reason for the menu change. If it was not motivated by concern about animal fat, it is not like the article in any way. Second, since we do not know the reason for the change, we do not know if the events are related or not. (B) The argument is not generalizing, but attempting to establish causation. It is trying to establish that the article brought about the menu change. In addition, we do not know if the events share any of the same characteristics. The first event is the publishing of an article showing concern about animal fats in the diet. The second is a menu change that might have been a response to shortages of animal fat to fry potatoes in. Therefore, instead of being of the same type, the events may be totally dissimilar. (C) Even if the menu change was a response to the article, the manager might have been told of it, instead of having read it himself. (D) This answer assumes that some reason has been given by the cafeteria for the switch. None was mentioned in the passage. The passage is not questioning the reason, but postulating a reason where none has been given. (E) This is the answer. Just because the article appeared yesterday and the menu change today, does not mean that the one caused the other. Any of a number of other factors could have caused the change.

22. **(B)** (A) The statements do not substantiate this. Just because the author can point to two untrained managers who have succeeded does not mean that training is always undesirable for managers. (B) The author is showing that, in some cases, lack of previous training was not a hindrance to on-the-job performance of managers. One may assume, then, that there are cases where such training is not necessary for success. It is possible that the director of corporation T is one of those who will succeed despite lack of training. He may be like the directors of corporations R and S in that respect. (C) This cannot be true, according to the information given in the passage. The passage cites two cases where managers succeeded despite lack of previous training. (D) Just because the passage cites three examples of corporate managers without training does not mean that the author assumes that few managers have such training. In fact, the author assumes the opposite. If few have such training it would not be necessary to argue that the director of corporation T may succeed despite lack of such training. (E) One would infer the opposite from the argument. If it is necessary to cite examples of some who have succeeded despite lack of training, it would appear that training is normally a prerequisite for success. Therefore, corporations would seek to hire those with previous training.

23. **(C)** (A) If past estimates have been low, present estimates may also be low. This means that the demand will probably be as great or greater than predicted. This is a good argument for going ahead with the project, not the opposite. (B) If energy shortages are still likely, they will be even more likely without the project. This is an argument in favor of the project. (C) This is the best answer. If alternate energy sources are available, perhaps they are less polluting and environmentally damaging than strip mining. They would then be preferable to strip mining. (D) If citizens have expressed no opinions, they may favor strip mining. This could, then, be in strip mining's favor. (E) While this may not be a good argument in favor of strip mining, it is also not an argument against it.

24. **(C)** This is an example of circular reasoning. The author argues that intelligent people choose one thing over another, and that act of choosing, by itself, makes them more intelligent. Look for the answer which duplicates this type of argument. (A) The word "intelligent" has at least this meaning in the passage: intelligence is something that enables one to make better choices. Therefore, (A) cannot be the answer, because it states that the term does not have any meaning. (B) The only thing that could be construed as an example is the choosing of one vacation spot over another. However, the passage cites no evidence to show that that choice is an intelligent one. Therefore, this example cannot establish the point that they are more intelligent for having made it. (C) This is exactly what the passage does. (D) and (E) are both plausible answers. However, they do not get the major flaw of the argument, which is circular reasoning.

25. **(E)** You are seeking an argument which asserts something as a fact, then attempts to prove it by asserting it again in a slightly altered form. (A) This is a valid form of the syllogism. It takes the following form: Homemakers prefer Vizz; homemakers are the best judges of home products; therefore, Vizz must be better. (B) This offers two reasons why Vizz is better: Homemakers prefer it; and it is useful in more than one type of chore. (C) This offers two reasons to show why oversized rackets are preferable: advanced players — who should be good judges of rackets — prefer them, and they have more power. (E) This tells you two things about Porsches: people with class like them, and they last longer. (E) This attempts to establish that Porsches are better by arguing that people with class drive them. But the only way you know that those people have class is that they drive Porsches. This is identical to the reasoning in the passages.

26. **(D)** This question asks you to look for the answer which (1) states a fact about the members of some group and (2) concludes that, because the fact is true of the individual members, it is true of the group which the members comprise. Answer (A) uses the opposite approach to what the question asks for. It concludes that a member of a group, Lynn, will be somewhere at a certain time, because the group as a whole is there at that time. Instead of extrapolating from a fact known about the members to a conclusion about the group, it extrapolates from the group to a particular member. (B) This answer draws no conclusions about Camaros as a whole, based on particular Camaros. It speaks only of a red Camaro and a blue one. (C) This answer states a fact about the group, chili, and draws a conclusion about the members based on that fact. This is just the opposite of what you are to look for. (D) This answer states a fact about the members of group, and draws a conclusion about the group based on that fact. Of course, the argument is flawed. But you were not asked to identify a flaw in the argument, but to identify a certain type of argument. (E) This answer draws a conclusion about Ed, a member of a group, based on a statement about the group as a whole.

Section 2 – Analytical Reasoning

QUESTIONS 1–5

Sample Diagrams

A: Players by Age   B: Roles by Age of Player

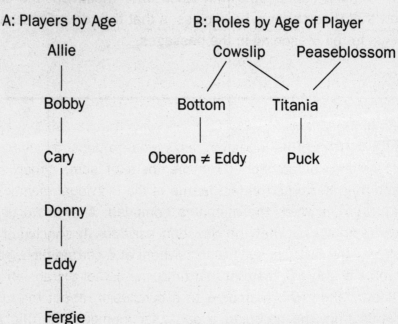

In the second diagram, those on different tracks (\ | /) are not ordered with respect to one another. Note: Only Peaseblossom and Cowslip can be played by Allie, the oldest, since everyone else is marked as younger than someone. Similarly, Fergie can play only Oberon or Puck.

---

1.   **(A)**   Revised Diagram B with information from this question.

```
          Cowslip
          Bottom
Oberon    Peaseblossom
          Titania
          Puck
```

Once Peaseblossom is said to be played by someone younger than someone else, only Cowslip is left to be played by the oldest, Allie. So, (A), that Allie plays Cowslip, must be right. Since Cowslip's player must be the oldest, it cannot be the second or third oldest (B) or (C) or any younger place (D). (E) is directly ruled out from the beginning, since whoever plays Cowslip must be older than the two who play Puck and Titania at least, and Eddy is older than only one person.

---

2.   (A)   This uses the original Diagram B.

(B) cannot be right because Titania has to be played by someone younger than the person playing Peaseblossom, so places four and five, at least, are reversed. Further, Peaseblossom cannot be played by Eddy, since whoever plays Peaseblossom has to be older than two other players and Eddy is older than only one. Eddy is also the reason (C) is wrong, for Eddy is explicitly said not to play Oberon, but that role is assigned Eddy in list (C). In list (D), Donny plays Puck, but Donny is older than Eddy, who plays Titania. Since Titania's player has to be older than Puck's, list (D) is ruled out. (E) fails because the person playing Bottom has to be younger than the one playing Cowslip - places 2 and 3, at least, are reversed in this list. This leaves (A) as the right answer and indeed (A) is possible. The order runs down the left side of diagram B and then down the right.

---

3.   (B)   Revised Diagram B using information from this question:

Cowslip
Bottom
Oberon
Peaseblossom
Puck

If Cary plays Oberon, then Cowslip and Bottom must be played by the two older players, in order, to satisfy the left side of Diagram B.

In particular, whoever plays Bottom has to be younger than someone - whoever plays Cowslip - and so cannot be the oldest, Allie. Thus, (A) must be wrong. But the person playing Bottom has to be younger than the oldest, Allie, but older than the person playing Oberon. Since that is Cary in this case, only Bobby can possibly fit in. So, (B) is right. Neither Donny nor Eddy can play Bottom since neither is older than Cary, the person playing Oberon. Thus, (C) and (D) are wrong. Finally, Fergie cannot play Bottom since there is someone younger than the Bottom player, namely, the Oberon player, but no one is younger than Fergie. Thus, (E) is wrong as well.

4.   **(C)**   This uses the original Diagram B.

The list (C) is not a possible ordering, since the person playing Puck has to be younger than the one playing Titania. Positions 3 and 5 in (C) are, thus, wrong. All of the other cases are possible. Nothing prevents Cowslip from being older than Peaseblossom or Titania from being younger than Oberon, so (A) satisfies the conditions. (D) is just (A) with a different, permitted, choice of which of the top two is to be first. In (B) and (E) pieces from one path in Diagram B are inserted into other paths at places where relative positions are not determined, so the results continues to satisfy the rules.

5.   **(C)**   Revised Diagram B, using information from this question

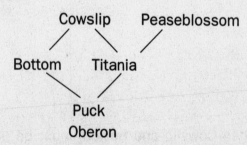

If Puck is played by the next to youngest, the youngest must play Oberon, since one of these two had to be played by the youngest. Thus, the person playing Puck must be younger than whoever plays Titania and the person playing Oberon is sure to be younger than whoever plays Bottom. Bobby cannot play Titania, however, since Bobby is next to the oldest and the person playing Titania is younger than the players of both Cowslip and Peaseblossom. Thus, (A) is not possible. On the other hand, if Fergie is Titania, then the youngest would be playing Titania, and it is stated that this person is older than Puck. This conflicts with the conditions, so (B) is not possible. If Donny is Titania, Allie, Bobby and Cary can divvy up Cowslip, Peaseblossom, and Bottom in a number of ways within the conditions laid down. Thus, (C) is the right answer. (D) and (E) fail because they are the oldest and the conditions state that the person playing Titania must be younger than two other people.

QUESTION 6-11

Initial Summary

Assuming each asked,
G: G i.e., G will be in the list
H: H <=> K i.e., H runs just in case K does
I: I <=> J
J: J <=> -G i.e., Janet's running implies G does not and conversely
K: K <=> -I
Anyone not asked does not run

6.　　**(C)**　　Since he was asked, George will run. Since George will run, Janet will not, since she and George cannot appear on the same slate. Thus, not all five will run, so (E) is incorrect. Since Janet will not run, neither will Irene, who will run only when Janet does. Thus, at least two of the five will not run, so it is not true that at least four will run. (D) is false. Since Irene will not run, Kay will run. Thus, at least 2 will run - George and Kay, so (A), that only one will run, is false. Since Kay will run, so will Henry, who runs (when asked) whenever Kay does. Thus, George, Kay and Henry will all run. This makes 3, so (C) is correct. It is more than 2, so (B) is wrong.

7.   **(C)**   Since George was not asked, he will not run. Janet was asked, though, and, so, she will run because George does not. That means at least one person will run and, so, (A) is wrong. Irene, in turn, will run because Janet will and that means at least two people will run, not just one. So, (B) is wrong as well. But Irene's running means that Kay will not run, since she will not run with Irene. Thus, at least two of the five will not run, and so (E) which says four will run, is wrong. Finally, Kay's not running prevents Henry from running. Thus, only Janet and Irene will run, exactly two people. So, (C) is the correct answer. (D) fails, of course, because Harry does not run and thus three of the five do not, meaning that fewer than three do.

8.   **(E)**   Janet was not asked and so will not run. But then, Irene will not run, even though asked, for she will not run without Janet. Thus, (B) and (E), which includes Irene among the candidates, is wrong. Since Irene will not run, Kay will. And, since Kay will run, so will Henry. Thus, just Kay and Henry will run. The fact that Kay runs means that (A), "only Henry" is wrong and similarly, the fact that Henry will run means that (C) is wrong. Thus, (E) is the right answer.

9.   **(A)**   George will run, because he was asked to. Janet was not asked to run, so she will not. But then, Irene will not run, for Janet will not. Thus, (C) and (D), which include Irene as a candidate, must be wrong. Kay will not run because she was not asked to. Consequently, Henry, though asked, will not run. (B) and (D), which have Henry as a candidate, are wrong. So, only George will run and only (A) is correct.

10.   **(B)**   If George was asked to run, he would. Consequently, Janet would not run even if she was asked to, for she never runs with George. But then, Irene, who will only run with Janet, would not run either. So, George and Irene cannot run together. (B) is correct. Continuing the same line of reasoning, starting with George running, since Irene does not run, Kay does, if asked, so George and Kay can serve together, needing only that they both are asked. So (C) is not a pair who cannot run together. And, if Kay runs and Henry is asked, he will run as well. Thus, neither (A) nor (D) is an impossible pair. Finally, if George is not asked, and so does not run, but Janet and Irene are asked, they will run together, Janet because George is not running and Irene because Janet is running. So (E) is also not an impossible pair.

11.   **(D)**   If George is asked to run, he will run. But if George runs, Janet will not. Since the committee wants Janet to run, the committee must not ask George. So, (A) which contains George will not achieve the desired result. Janet will also not run if she is not asked, so (C), which does not ask Janet to run, will not work. Henry will not run if Kay does not and Kay will not run if not asked, so, since the committee wants Henry to run, it must ask Kay. Thus, plans (A), (B) and (E), which do not ask Kay, will not work. This leaves plan (D), which will work: Janet will run because Irene will not (for the same reason). But then Henry will run as well, since Kay does.

12.   **(C)**   To get the largest number in, begin with the smallest and build up until capacity is reached. The total capacity is six tons or 12,000 pounds. So, one crate weighing 1,000 pounds can go in, giving a total of 1,000 pounds. Look at totals after various additions (in 1,000 pound units)

total crates	#/weight	weight	total weight
1	1 @ 1	1	1
3	2 @ 2	4	5
6	3 @ 3	9	14

This is too much, but not putting all of the last group in gives

5	2 @ 3	6	11

So, a total of five crates can be stowed, answer (C). Clearly, using any of the heavier crates will allow no more crates to be stowed. Using only one of the 3,000 pound crates and 1 of the 4,000 pounders would still permit only five crates, though it would bring the total weight up to 12,000 pounds.

As for the other answers, the chart above shows a way to have only three crates aboard and still have room for more (1 @ 1 and 2 @ 2 leaves room for 2 @ 3), so (A) is wrong. Similarly, (B) is shown wrong by the possibility of having four crates consisting of 1 @ 1, 2 @ 2, 1 @ 3 and still having room for 1 @ 3 or even 1 @ 4. (D) fails because the lightest possible using 6 crates is the combination listed first above and that weighs more than is available. Finally, (E) fails since it must inevitably weigh even more than a combination of six crates and that is already more than allowed.

---

13.   **(B)**   To find the minimum number, start with the heaviest, in this case, the 4,000-pound crates. Three of them will exactly fill the 12,000 pound limit, so answer (B) is correct. Using lighter crates will require more crates to come up to the required weight. (A) has to be wrong, for the most that two crates could weigh is 8,000 pounds (2 @ 4,000) which is less than the amount allowed. The remaining cases fail because five is the maximum number of crates that can be stowed.

14. **(D)** Given that 3 @ 3,000, i.e., 9,000 pounds, are stowed, only 3,000 pounds remain. With the crates available, the maximum number to fill that space would be

```
1    @ 1  1    1
1    @ 2  2    3
```

So, two more crates could be gotten on. The fact that this is possible means that (E), only one more crate, does not represent the maximum. On the other hand, any combination involving more crates will weigh more than the permitted amount. (A), (B), and (C) must, then, all be wrong. In addition, each of these would involve more than five crates being stowed (the 3 @ 3 plus the addition number > 2) and five is the maximum number of crates which could be stowed.

15. **(D)** Except for the two-ton crates, all the crates cost $10 per 1,000 pounds to ship. The two-ton crates cost less per 1,000 pounds. So, the maximum shipping charge would come from shipping 12,000 pounds at the higher rate, i.e., $120 total, answer (D). The purser could reach full capacity at this rate in several ways, for example one 1,000-pound crate, one 2,000-pound crate, and three 3,000-pound crates. (A) gives the rate for full capacity at the lower rate, three 2-ton crates @ $25. But the higher rate is available and gives a larger total charge. (B) could be reached by using two two-ton crates and two one-ton ones, but still uses part of the lower rate and so does not maximize the total charge. (C) is probably the result of not putting on a full six tons of cargo, using perhaps one 1,000-pound crate, two one-ton crates, and two one-and-a-half-ton crates – the maximum number but not the maximum tonnage allowed, and so not as high a charge as possible. (E) is not a possible charge at all, since even at the higher rate, it would require 15,000 pounds of cargo and there are only 12,000 available.

16. **(B)** The guaranteed total would be the minimum obtainable under the condition that he use at least 6,000 pounds. Since, except for the cheaper two-ton crates, crates go for $10 per 1,000 pounds, this total must be at most $60, i.e., all 6,000 pounds at the highest rate. But it is possible to take some of this tonnage in two-ton crates at the lower rate, so $60 is not the minimum under the conditions and (E) is wrong. In particular, the purser could lead one two-ton crate at $25 and one one-ton crate at $20 for a total of $45 dollars in charges for three tons. So, (C) and (D) are also not minimum charges. On the other hand, there is no way to get down to $40 without taking on less than three tons, for, at the higher rate, $40 would only pay for two tons of freight, while the lower rate only applies to units of two tons each, one of which would be $25 but too light and two of which would be $50 and also too heavy. The nearest combinations of rates would be a two-ton crate and a 1,000-pound crate, which would be only $35 and would be too light or the two-ton and the one-ton which give the actual minimum noted. So, (A) does not give a minimum for the given conditions.

QUESTIONS 17–21

Original set up of the schematic

Black Player

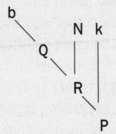

White Player

Only items connected by lines are placed correctly relative to one another, except that position relative to the White Queen – left or right, nearer to or farther from the White Player is also set.

17. **(C)** The White King is given as nearer the White Player than the White Queen, so the cases which place it farther away, (B) and (E), must be wrong. The diagram above shows that four pieces are to the right of the White Queen and it is given that twice as many pieces are to the right as to the left of the White Queen. So, there must be at least two pieces to the left of the White Queen. Only the Black Bishop is shown on the left and only the White King remains to be placed, so it must be on the left as well. So, the White King lies toward the White Player from the White Queen and to the left, (C). The fact that there are only six pieces besides the White Queen on the board and that are divided into those left and those right of the White Queen, with all accounted for, means that none are in the same column as the White Queen. Thus, neither (A) nor (B) can be correct. The fact that the White King must be to the left of the White Queen, as argued above, means that (D) and (E), which have it to the right of the White Queen, are not correct.

The final chart must be:

Black Player

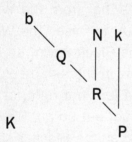

White Player

---

18. **(A)** Only the Black Bishop, White Knight, and Black King are beyond the White Queen, so only the Black Bishop and White Knight could be on the same row as the Black King, since all on the row must be the same distance from the White edge. Thus, (D) and (E), which say that there are three or four items on that row, must be wrong. Black King is in the same column as the Black Pawn and the

Black Bishop is diagonally to the left and away from the Black Pawn, so the Black Bishop must also be to the left, not right, of the Black King. So, only the White Knight could be to the right of the Black King and (C), which says that two items might be, is wrong. But the White Knight is in the same column as the White Rook, which is to the left and away from the Black Pawn. The White Knight is thus to the left of the Black Pawn and so also of the Black King. So even the White Knight is not to the right of the Black King. Thus, (B) is wrong, for not even one piece is to the right of the Black King. So, (A), that no pieces are to the right of the Black King, is correct.

---

19.   **(E)**   The White Knight is in the same column as the White Rook and the White Rook is to the left of (and away from) the Black Pawn, so the White Knight is to the left of the Black Pawn. But the Black King is in the same column as the Black Pawn, so the White Knight is also to the left of the Black King. Thus, the claim in (E) has to be true. On the other hand, the White Rook is farther from the White Player than the Black Pawn (and to the left), so (A) is false. The White Queen is on the left and away diagonally from the Black Pawn, so it is to the left of the Black Pawn. But the Black King is in the same column as the Black Pawn, so the White Queen is to the left, not right, of the Black King and (D) is false. (B) and (C) may be true, but do not have to be. The White King is nearer to the White Player than the Black Bishop, but is not located left to right relative to the Black Bishop, so it is false that (C) must be true. Similarly, the Black Pawn is clearly to the right of the White King but is not located relative to it in distance from the White Player, so (B) does not have to be true.

---

20.   **(C)**   Nearer to the Black Player means farther from the White Player. So the White Queen, which is nearer to the White Player than the Black Bishop, cannot be also nearer to the Black Player. This goes also for the pieces nearer to the White Player than the White

Queen: the White King, the White Rook, and the Black Pawn. Thus, including the Black Bishop itself, five pieces CANNOT be nearer the Black Player than the Black Bishop. This means that at most 2 can be, so (A) and (B) are wrong. The two possibilities are the White Knight and the Black King, both of which are, like the Black Bishop, are farther from the White Player – so they are nearer to the Black Player – than the White Queen. But all that can be inferred for sure about these in relation to the Black Bishop is that they are right of it, from the White Player's point of view, not which is nearer to or farther from the White Player. Thus, both might be nearer the Black Player than the Bishop. So, (C) is the correct answer. Either (D) or (E) might be the number that actually are closer in a given case, for either or both of the White Knight and Black King could be as far or father from the Black Player as the Bishop, but none of these has to be true, so (C) may be, which is what is asked for.

21. **(D)** Because they are farther along the leftward diagonal from the Black Pawn than the White Rook, both the White Queen and the Black Bishop must be left of the White Rook. Thus, at least two pieces must be left of the White Rook and (A) and (B), which say that fewer than two are wrong. Further, since the White King is to the left of the White Queen, which is to the left of the White Rook, the White King is to the left of the White Rook as well. Thus, three pieces must be left of the White Rook, and (C), which says that at most two are, is wrong. On the other hand, the Black Pawn is before the White Rook on the leftward diagonal and, so, is not left of the White Rook. The Black King is in the same column as the Black Pawn and so no farther left than the Black Pawn and thus also not left of the White Rook. Finally, the White Knight is in the same column as the White Rook and thus exactly as far left as the White Rook, so not left of the White Rook. Thus, there cannot be four left of the White Rook and (E) is false. But three are definitely left of the White Rook, so (D) is correct.

QUESTIONS 22–26

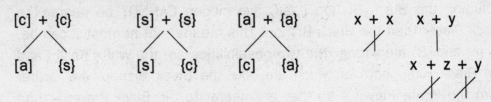

22. **(A)** Only Smoke cavies produce male offspring of the same color as the parents, so (A) must be right. Coal cavies produce neither offspring the same color as the parents, so (B) and (E) must be wrong. And (C) is wrong, because male offspring of an Ash pair are Coal, not Ash. (D) fails for the same reason as (C).

---

23. **(D)** The possible sequences of generations are {c}-[s]-{c}, {s}-[c]-{s}, and {a}-[a]-{a}. The other three patterns at the second generation result and a granddaughter of a different color from the grandmother: {c}-[a]-{a}, {s}-[s]-{c}, and {a}-[c]-{s}. What all the successful ones have in common is that the middle member is also female, i.e., that the granddaughter is the older's daughter's daughter, (D). The second (and third) patterns above show that (A) is false and the first and third show that (B) is false also. The three failing patterns all show that the middle link cannot be male, i.e., that (C) is false. And the first and second patterns — the no-Ash pairs — show that (E) is false.

Section 3 – Reading Comprehension

1. **(C)** This question requires the test-taker to pick the primary purpose of the passage. The passage begins by suggesting the courts have not received sufficient scientific scrutiny because they have not been viewed as political bodies. The passage continues by noting the traditional use of case analysis. The author argues that this method has too narrow a focus and does not allow one to see the broader aspects of the workings of courts. The author admits that case studies have some merit, but advocates broader, more scientific, studies. (C) is correct because the first two sentences of the passage suggest that the judiciary is not studied properly. Next the author describes why the judiciary is studied, using the case analysis method, then continues by pointing out the problems of this method. The author concludes the passage by suggesting greater benefits would occur if the judiciary were studied differently. (A) is incorrect because by stating it is a "myth that judges are nonpolitical arbiters of the law" (fourth paragraph), the author shows a belief that judges are political, and notes most judicial scholars are also aware that judges are political actors. The assertion by the author that judges are political actors is only one piece of evidence in support of his more general thesis. (B) is incorrect because the author clearly states, "[t]his is not to say the judicial branch has lacked all scrutiny, only that it has traditionally been viewed from a perspective different from the other two branches of government" (first paragraph). (D) is incorrect because very little information on the case analysis method is given. It is mentioned only as supporting evidence for the broader proposition that study of the judiciary must be more scientific. (E) is also incorrect. As with response (D), the passage only mentions judicial review in passing. The mention of judicial review is used only to give an example of how the cult of the robe has led people to view judges as being nonpolitical.

2.   **(B)**   Marshall's conclusion is that judges should interpret the Constitution because they are nonpolitical. This suggests whether decision makers are political makes a difference in how they interpret the Constitution. Marshall's assumption in choosing the courts for this task is that political actors such as executives and legislatures cannot be impartial. (A) is incorrect because there is no mention in the passage of education levels. The reference to qualifications in the passage concerns whether the decision makers are politically motivated, not how well educated they are. (C) is incorrect because there is no mention that Marshall believed judges to have a greater understanding of the Constitution. Again, Marshall emphasized the *political* differences between judges and other members of government. (D) is incorrect because Marshall's statements do not relate to the study of the judiciary. Marshall was concerned with interpretation of the Constitution. It is the author of the passage who is concerned with the study of the judiciary. The author only uses Marshall's comments as an example of the kind of thinking which led to the emphasis on studying individual cases. (E) is incorrect. As with (D), Marshall's comments do not pertain to the use of precedent. His comments are concerned with the *who* of interpreting the Constitution, not the *how*.

3.   **(E)**   The phrase *cult of the robe* is introduced immediately after Marshall's comments on the inability of the politically motivated branches of government to be nonpolitical arbiters of the Constitution (first paragraph). The author directly links Marshall's comments to the cult of the robe by saying his comments are "a classic example" of these beliefs. (A) is incorrect because the cult of the robe is shown to be a belief in the neutrality of judges, not a particular method of interpreting the Constitution. (B) is incorrect for the same reason as (A). In addition, it is *stare decisis* which is the *use* of past cases, not the cult of the robe. (C) is incorrect. The author argues that the cult of the robe has *influenced* the study of the courts, but it is not itself a method of study. (D) is incorrect. The author makes clear that the use of individual cases in decision making, or the use of precedent, is "known in legal terms as *stare decisis*" (third paragraph).

4. **(D)** In the third and fourth paragraphs the author argues belief in the cult of the robe has led to a reliance on the case analysis method. In the fourth and fifth paragraphs the author argues this method is inadequate. (A) is incorrect because the author argues that the cult of the robe is a myth. The author also indicates "judicial scholars by and large do not subscribe to the myth" (fourth paragraph). (B) is incorrect because the author is not contrasting the advantages of *stare decisis* and the cult of the robe. In addition, as mentioned in the explanation to question three, the cult is not a method, but the belief that judges are nonpolitical. (C) is incorrect because the author notes that most judicial scholars do not subscribe to the myth of the cult of the robe (fourth paragraph). The author continues by arguing that even though researchers do not believe the myth, they still focus on judicial biographies and case studies. Thus, according to the author, researchers are not being misled, but are also not properly studying the courts. (E) is incorrect because just the opposite has occurred. The author is suggesting there is too much study of individual cases, which follows from the belief that judges are nonpolitical arbiters of the law (second paragraph).

5. **(A)** The paraphrase of Wieland suggests that by concentrating on the details of individual cases, researchers lose sight of the broader workings of courts. This fits the author's overall theme that broader studies of the courts must be undertaken. (B) is incorrect. The author is not suggesting courts are organic entities, or that they are trees. The reference to Wieland's statement about trees is intended as a metaphor for the consequences of examining something in minute detail. (C) is incorrect. Other parts of the passage do argue that judges are political, but the reference to Wieland does not. At this stage in the passage the author has already provided evidence of the cult of the robe, and how it has led to the traditional study of individual cases. In referring to Wieland, the author is suggesting that one loses sight of the greater whole when concentrating on individual cases. (D) is incorrect. Precedent, *per se*, is not a problem. The author says so in the reference to Joyce Kilmer by saying, metaphorically, that there is value in examining individual cases. According to the author, the problem is the *exclusive* reliance on precedent. It is for this reason the author advocates broader studies of courts (A). (E) is incorrect. The case analysis method relies on the study of individual cases. In referring to Wieland, the author is suggesting that something is lost or missing by only concentrating on the details (individual cases).

---

6.   **(D)**   In the preceding reference to Wieland, the author suggests something is lost or missing by concentrating only on individual cases. Nevertheless, in referring to Kilmer, the author suggests that the study of individual cases does have some merit. (A) is incorrect because the passage does not address the question of the beauty of studying courts. It can be assumed that the author feels the study of courts has merit. The reference to beauty, however, metaphorically suggests that there is value in studying individual cases. (B) is incorrect. The author is concerned about too much emphasis on individual *cases,* but the author does not mention individual *courts.* (C) is incorrect. As noted above, the reference to Kilmer is intended to recognize there is some merit in studying individual cases, but this does not mean researchers should *rely* on them. Attaching such a meaning to the Kilmer reference would make the author's arguments contradictory. (E) is incorrect. The author recognizes "judicial scholars by and large do not subscribe to the myth that judges are nonpolitical arbiters of the law" (fourth paragraph), so it is unnecessary to discourage belief in the cult. In addition, as with (C), if (E) were true it would lead to a contradictory argument by the author.

---

7.   **(C)**   This is the point of the Wieland reference. The author is arguing for broader studies of courts rather than narrowly focused biographies and case studies. (A) is incorrect. Although it may be true that every case is different in some regard, this is not the problem the author is addressing. The author is concerned with the method of studying cases, not the cases themselves. (B) is incorrect. The author's concern is not with recognition of the political aspects of courts. The author recognizes that most judicial scholars do not believe judges are nonpolitical actors (fourth paragraph). Nevertheless, the author believes there to be undue reliance on case studies in judicial research, so the problem is not with recognition of the political aspects of courts. (D) is incorrect for the same reasons as (B). The cult of the robe is mentioned merely to show what led to the current reliance on case studies and judicial biographies. The author does not believe the cult of the robe to be a current problem (fourth paragraph). (E) is incorrect. The author specifically rejects any suggestion that the details should be ignored by stating, "One must remain cognizant of the details" (third paragraph).

---

8. **(A)** The author recognizes some value in the study of individual cases (fourth paragraph), but argues that such studies cannot grasp the broader aspects of how courts work. Thus, the author is skeptical as to the value of relying solely on individual case studies. (B) is incorrect. Although the author does recognize there is some value in case studies (fourth paragraph), the author's argument centers on the belief they are used too often. The author is unsupportive of continued *reliance* on case studies for judicial analysis. (C) is incorrect. The point of the passage is to argue for more broad-based studies and less reliance on case studies. It cannot, therefore, be said the author's attitude toward case studies is neutral. (D) is incorrect. The author recognizes there is some value in case studies and judicial biographies (fourth paragraph). The author is not disdainful of such studies, only concerned that they dominate judicial research and fail to capture the broader aspects of courts. (E) is incorrect. Indifference suggests not caring about case studies and judicial biographies. The author does care about them. The value of such studies is specifically noted (fourth paragraph). In addition, the author's argument centers on the belief that such studies are used too much in judicial research. Thus, it cannot be said the author is indifferent to case studies and judicial biographies.

9. **(C)**   The author specifically mentions strong leadership four times in the passage: (1) the death of Harold left no one able to successfully organize a resistance, (2) the election of Edgar to provide a symbol of unity, (3) the submission of the English lords to William because he was a strong leader, and (4) England's increased resistance to foreign rule when William left the country. The passage certainly describes some of William's exploits, but not in sufficient quantity or depth to be considered a chronicle. Thus, (A) is incorrect. (B) is also incorrect. Although the passage does suggest the importance of London, it does so only as one point in a broader theme. The author uses the fall of London to show how English lords were impressed with strong leadership. (D) is incorrect because the author seems to recognize William's presence was needed there as well (perhaps a fifth reference to strong leadership). The author merely notes William's absence from England caused additional resistance without making a judgment about the decision to leave. (E) is incorrect because the author *emphasizes* the importance of Harold's death. Without Harold, there was no one of sufficient ability left to organize and lead England's defense.

10. **(B)**   The author specifically notes the English lords rallied their surviving forces in London to resist William's advance. Thus, (E) is incorrect. We are told that William's assault on London bridge failed and he realized he did not have the equipment to storm London. This shows (A) to be incorrect. William did not give up on London and turn to other parts of England, as (D) suggests. Instead he laid waste to the area surrounding London, cutting it off from supplies and reinforcements (B). Although the Anglo-Saxon lords did meet with William and surrender to him, these were peace talks and cannot be considered treachery, making (C) incorrect.

11. **(D)** The author emphasizes the importance of strong leadership throughout the passage. The implication is that William should have realized this as well. By killing England's only strong leader and being a strong leader himself, he was able to conquer England and become its king. It is thus ironic that William's strong leadership gained him two kingdoms, *both* of which required his presence. The author does not suggest William's return to Normandy was based on a whim or otherwise unnecessary (A), nor does he suggest it was for administrative purposes (E). The fact a resistance was organized in William's absence means it *was* of consequence (C). The author certainly feels the decision to return to Normandy was not unimportant. Nevertheless, it was not a key element in England's resistance effort. The length of time William spent putting down resistance efforts (eight years) does not suggest if he had stayed there would have been no attempt to resist foreign rule.

12. **(A)** The last sentence of the passage makes (A) the clear answer by suggesting resistance to foreign rule was more important than the poor leadership skills of William's lieutenants. It is true that William needed to delegate administrative duties, but the more important consideration is English resistance to foreign rule. The degree of resistance William faced suggests even benevolent and diplomatic lieutenants would have met resistance eventually. (C) and (D) are both clearly wrong. In the last paragraph we are told that William did leave England to return to his duchy. In addition, there would be no point in noting English resistance to foreign rule if William was from England. The harsh rule of William's lieutenants probably forced him to return to England much sooner than he expected or preferred, so it was important. The remaining portion of (E) is pure speculation not supported by the passage.

13. **(B)**   As (B) suggests, the author says, "They immediately elected as king Edgar ... to provide a symbol of resistance and unity." Although Edgar was a Saxon, as was Harold, there is no suggestion in the passage that Edgar was a descendant of Harold's (D), nor that Edgar's heritage was of significance apart from serving as a rallying point. Thus, (A) is also incorrect. The purpose of electing Edgar king was to rally English forces to defeat William. There is no suggestion in the passage electing Edgar king would in any way prevent William's ascension to the throne other than his possible military defeat — which did not occur (C). There is also no mention of constitutional requirements which makes (E) irrelevant.

14. **(E)**   The author notes that after the death of Harold there was a willingness to resist, but "no leadership to call it forth." Recognizing this lack of leadership and the strong leadership of William makes it clear the death of Harold signals the fall of England. This makes (A) wrong, and (B) wrong simply because there was no strong English leader. There is no suggestion in the passage that the English planned to mount a counteroffensive in Normandy or had allies there who would. The entire passage is concerned with events in England, thus making (D) incorrect. Although the author notes Stigand, the Archbishop of Canterbury, was the first to submit to William, the implication seems to be that this was merely the first of what would eventually be many. There is no indication the archbishop was a determining factor in the fate of England (C).

15. **(D)**   The author notes after his victory in London and ascension to the throne, "William strengthened his hold upon the new land." (A) is incorrect because William returned to Normandy three months after being crowned, and only after he felt he was in sufficient control. The passage begins with the battle of Hastings where Harold was defeated, and then William advanced on London. Thus, (B) is incorrect. (C) is wrong because we are told it was the resistance of

Kentishmen which forced William to return to England from Normandy. (E) is wrong because Edgar was defeated at London, and also because Saxony is not part of England.

---

16. **(B)** The author begins the passage by suggesting absolute moral rules are implausible. He then provides evidence and examples leading to the conclusion that they are also impossible to maintain. (A) is incorrect because the discussion of Dutch fishermen is only mentioned as an example of how two absolute moral rules can come into conflict, forcing the actors (the Dutch fishermen in the example) to violate at least one of two absolute rules. The author does point out a difference between Kant and Geach, but this difference is not central to the passage (C). The author mentions the difference to show how each philosopher deals with the possibility of conflicting absolute moral rules and then refutes each position. The author is not arguing against moral rules in general, nor is their inconsistency of paramount concern (D). The problem, according to the author, is the *absoluteness* of the rules. This is emphasized in the last sentence of the passage. The consideration of hypothetical philosophical problems (E) is used to show how absolute moral rules can come into conflict. The hypotheticals are used as examples only, and are not the central focus of the passage.

---

17. **(E)** The author notes Geach's position at the end of the second paragraph: "God will not permit such circumstances to exist in the real world." One may invent fictitious conflicts, but, according to Geach, since absolute moral rules are divine commands, God would not allow a conflict to arise in the real world. The passage makes no mention of how Geach would explain the case of the Dutch fishermen (A), or the Inquiring Murderer (D). (B) is clearly the opposite of Geach's position. The author makes it clear in the second paragraph that although both Kant and Geach believe in absolute moral rules, their reasons are very different (C).

18. **(A)**   The passage mentions The Case of the Inquiring Murderer, but does not tell us what it is about. Nevertheless, the author does indicate in the first sentence that it serves as an argument against absolute moral rules. In the third paragraph the author indicates the example of the Dutch fishermen provides a real example which makes the same point as that of the Inquiring Murderer; more than one absolute moral rule raises the possibility of conflict. We can deduce that The Case of the Inquiring Murderer also illustrates the possibility of conflict. Given the author's description of the two cases in the third paragraph (B) cannot be correct. The Case of the Inquiring Murderer is used to argue *against* absolute moral rules. Thus, (D) is incorrect, as is (C), since Geach supports the existence of absolute moral rules. (E) is incorrect because the author specifically states The Case of the Inquiring Murderer is fictitious.

19. **(B)**   The author's purpose is to argue against absolute moral rules. He cannot, therefore, believe Kant's position which supports their existence. This makes (A) incorrect, as well as (D). Given the effort the author spends refuting Kant's position, it cannot be said that he is indifferent to it (C). Nevertheless, the author gives no indication that he thinks Kant's position is stupid, trivial, or otherwise deserving of disdain (E). He merely disagrees with Kant's position and attempts to prove it wrong.

20. **(A)**   As noted in the explanation to question 17, Geach believes absolute moral rules to be of divine origin, and God will not permit conflict to actually arise. Geach may find hypotheticals interesting, but nevertheless irrelevant to the real world. By arguing God will not permit conflict to occur in the real world, Geach must recognize that examples of hypothetical conflict do exist, making (B) incorrect. Geach's position is not that examples of hypothetical conflict are unlikely to occur (C). It is that God will not allow them to occur. (D) is incorrect because it is clear from the passage that although Geach recognizes the existence of examples of hypothetical conflict between absolute moral rules, he still believes they exist. (E) is incorrect because Kant's position supports absolute moral rules and the hypotheticals argue against them, and because there is no mention in the passage of Geach commenting on Kant's position.

---

21. **(C)** The author states this directly in the last paragraph to explain why Kant's defense is untenable. It is also in this last paragraph where the author rejects the possibility that if two absolute moral rules exist they will not come into conflict (A). The author feels Kant's defense, which is (E), is weak and cannot explain every possibility. (B) is more in line with Geach's position. The author provides a real world example of conflict by discussing the Dutch fishermen. (D) is incorrect because Geach's position raises a different defense, that of divine intervention.

---

22. **(A)** The passage begins by indicating the implausibility of absolute moral rules. It continues by presenting arguments, and eventually concluding, that they are also impossible to maintain. (B) is incorrect because the author is not denouncing Kant, merely trying to show why he is wrong with regard to absolute moral rules. Other writings by Kant are neither mentioned nor relevant. Geach's position may raise questions of free will versus determinism (C), but the author does not raise the issue in his arguments. The author's example of the Dutch fishermen (D) is just that, an example. It is used in support of the basic argument, but it is not the argument itself, i.e., the author is not trying to prove something about Dutch fishermen. The author's position against absolute moral rules makes (E) clearly wrong.

23.   **(B)**   The author describes the biological clock of the horseshoe crab with the conclusion that its brain transmits signals to its eye to allow it to see at night. The author then suggests that this finding may help to explain how humans see. (A) is incorrect because the author recognizes much work has been done on the horseshoe crab by showing surprise that the crab's biological clock has not been discovered before. (C) is wrong because the author begins the passage by noting the simplicity of the crab's visual system, and concludes by noting how complex the human visual system is. The author does briefly mention two types of neural connections associated with visual systems, but the point of the reference is how they are part of a visual system (D). The author finds it interesting that this discovery was only recently made with regard to a visual system which is one of the most thoroughly studied. From the importance the author places on the study we can assume the author would not argue the visual system of the crab is too simple to warrant further study (E).

24.   **(E)**   This is stated in the first sentence of the third paragraph. (A) is incorrect because it is not the nocturnal activities of horseshoe crabs which interests the author, but how the crabs can adapt to changes in light levels. Human inability to see at night is only briefly mentioned in counterpoint to the ability of crabs. There is no indication in the passage that the author has also studied human visual systems (B). (C) is incorrect because it is what the author *discovered* while studying the horseshoe crab. In the first sentence of the passage the author seems to imply that the crab's visual system is no longer thought to be primitive. In addition, according to the author's statement in paragraph three, the point of his study was not the crab's visual system *per se*, but how the system adapted to different light levels. Thus, (D) is incorrect.

25. **(C)**   The passage is describing how the horseshoe crab's visual system adapts to changing light levels. The author does not make any reference to artificial lighting, so we can assume the changes are natural and follow the normal 24-hour day. The author does note the great age of *Limulus* (the horseshoe crab), but this has nothing to do with its biological clock (except, perhaps, that it took that long to develop) (A). (B) is incorrect because there is no mention in the passage as to whether the crab sleeps. Mention of biological clocks in humans often refer to the fact women stop producing eggs later in life. In this passage, however, the reference concerns how the crab's visual system has adapted to daily changes from light to dark, not its reproductive system (D). The passage does not compare the cycles of humans and birds to that of the crab. The noted difference in the ability to see at night is a difference in what occurs during the cycle, not the cycle itself. Thus, (E) is also incorrect.

26. **(A)**   In the third paragraph the author specifically notes the importance of discovering the 24-hour biological clock in the crab. There is no indication in the passage that the author had any hand in determining the age of the species (E). In the first sentence of the last paragraph the author admits no one knows how people see, thus making (C) incorrect. Similarly, it is the author's *hope* that his discovery of the crab's adaptive system will aid in the study of the visual system of birds, but this has not yet occurred (B). (D) is incorrect because there is no indication in the passage that the human visual system is in any way related to that of the crab.

27. **(D)**   In the fourth and fifth paragraphs the author describes efferent and afferent connections. The fourth paragraph discusses two-way connections, then the fifth begins with the phrase "Similar efferent connections" from which we can deduce that efferent connections are two-way connections. (A) is wrong because there is no mention of the crab's anatomy or physical appearance. (B) is incorrect because the first sentence of the fifth paragraph specifically indicates these connections have been found in animals other than birds. If any such timer exists, it does so in the crab's brain, as we are told in the third paragraph. The discussion of efferent connections concerns how the information from the brain and timer reaches the eyes. Thus, (C) is incorrect. The passage is concerned with why crabs can see at night, not why humans cannot. From the passage we can gather it is the brain which controls whether humans or crabs can see at night. The efferent connections only carry the information. Thus (E) is incorrect.

28.   **(A)**   This is the point of the author's last paragraph. Given the time the author has devoted to the study of the visual system of the crab and his hope that his discovery will help to explain more complex visual systems it would be wrong to conclude the author's study is of little importance (B). (C) is incorrect because the author does not attempt to explain *why* horseshoe crabs have survived so long, only that they have. There is no mention in the passage of why or how evolution takes place, and there is no indication that further study will do so (D). (E) is incorrect because just the opposite has occurred with respect to the crab. The crab's visual system was considered very simple, but the author discovered it to be more complex than originally thought.

Section 4 –
Logical Reasoning

1. **(C)** The writer *concludes* that it is all right to eat fish (C), on the *premise* that fish eat other fish (A). This is contrary to his previous views that it is murder to eat fish (B) and that we should not eat animal food (E). He apparently thought about changing his mind because the fish smelled appetizing in the frying pan (D).

2. **(B)** The speaker refers to John and himself as "we," as though they were both equal (B). It is not John, but the others that the speaker regards as servants (C) and that he claims to own (A). Since the passage simply states the speaker's opinion, we cannot decide whether the speaker really owns everything (D) or whether John does not enjoy anything (E).

3. **(B)** The writer's conclusion is that the subjects of the passage were not impressed with death. Hence, it would be inconsistent to suggest that these people were impressed by death (B). As support for his conclusion, the writer cites the cemeteries' surfaces' displaying bones (A), the familiarity of these people with the dead (C) and with the idea of their own death (D), and the analogy of the skull in *Hamlet* (E).

4. **(D)** The writer rejects the view that we should never take a critical position toward another culture. Hence, this view's assertion is contrary to, not a premise for, the writer's conclusion (D). As premises for rejection of this view, the writer asserts that we cannot respect what we do not find intelligible (A), respect implies a favorable judgment (B), and a favorable judgment implies knowledge of the object of judgment (C). And the writer implies that moral isolationism is not respectful (E), since it fails to meet the requirements of the premises.

---

5. **(C)**   The passage claims that Yeltsin has taken the lead thanks to Gorbachev's turn to the right, not Yeltsin's own turn (C). The passage identifies Gorbachev, not Yeltsin, as the Soviet President (A), denies that Yeltsin and Gorbachev may reconcile (B), claims that Gorbachev is divorced from the reform camp (D), and names Yeltsin, not Gorbachev, as the uncontested leader of the U.S.S.R. (E).

---

6. **(A)**   The hospital officials' conclusion is that the risk of a patient contracting HIV from an infected surgeon is low. This conclusion would be strengthened if the only reported case of a patient being infected by a surgeon turns out to be false, (A). It is impossible to judge the relevance of the information on health care workers becoming infected, since we are not told if any of them are surgeons, or how they became infected. Perhaps all of them are lab technicians, who became infected by handling blood and tissue samples, and who never came into direct contact with patients. Therefore, (B) and (C) can be eliminated. That the dentist was never tested for HIV is irrelevant, since the passage admits that the report of his infecting a patient is unconfirmed. It is irrelevant whether or not Bartlett is a surgeon at Hopkins, since his authority for the statement in the passage rests on his being the director of the Hopkins AIDS program.

7. **(D)** The writer implies that Einstein's and Bach's mental abilities go beyond mere electrical processes and that advances in science and technology may help us to understand this (D). This contradicts the assertion that a mind is nothing but electrical processes (C). The premises are that there are heretofore unimagined perceptions (B) of the microcosm and macrocosm; that these perceptions, not the microcosm and macrocosm themselves, have become commonplace (A); and that these perceptions are due to the scientific and technological advances of the telescope, the microscope, and space travel (E).

8. **(E)** The writer's conclusion is about the *Today* show's problem — based on the premises that Gumbel has alienated female viewers and that Gumbel's Q score is low (E). The writer states (but not as a conclusion) that Gumbel is in trouble and is a problem because his Q score is low, not because female viewers have alienated him (A) or because the *Today* show has made major moves (D). He also asserts that the *Today* show is suffering because young female audiences are worse, not that the audience is worse because the show is suffering (C). And the writer claims that Gumbel is an able broadcaster *in spite of* his low Q score, not because of it (B).

9. **(B)** If the Eternal is unchangeable, but wisdom about past events may change from old man to young man to grown man, then such wisdom must not be eternal (B). The passage claims that statements about the changeable, not about the Eternal (A) are subject to change. The passage claims that the Eternal applies to every human being, contrary to answer (C). The passage also states that youth cannot, and grown men do not, wish to understand wisdom about the past, but it says nothing about understanding wisdom in general (D) and (E).

10.   (D)   The writer *denies* the proposition that only by legal restraints are men to be kept from aggressing on their neighbors (D). Thus, he attempts to support the claim that we should qualify the assumption of that proposition (B). As support he asserts that (1) debts of honor cannot be enforced legally (A), but are nevertheless more sacred than debts that can be legally enforced (E); and (2) formally registered contracts are not necessarily safer than contracts made between two Stock Exchange brokers who note the contracts in their notebooks (C).

---

11.   (A)   The passage concludes that knowledge in A.D. 3000 should surpass current understanding of aesthetics, psychology, and value. He does not claim that current understanding is pitiful now (A), so this is not a premise. He does claim or imply as premises that it would be bad if knowledge did not improve (B), that our powers are rapidly developing (C), that we should be able to guide these powers (D), and that for many people rapid development of our own powers is their chief interest of existence (E).

---

12.   (E)   The magician's *premises* are that like produces like (The Law of Similarity) (A) and things which have been in contact continue ever afterwards to act on each other (The Contact of Contagion) (D). From these the magician infers the *conclusions* that he can produce any effect he desires (B) and whatever he does to a material object will automatically affect the person with whom it was once in contact (C). Thus, both (A) and (D) are premises (E), while neither (B) nor (C) is a premise.

13. **(E)** The passage disagrees with the editor's claim that there is a new orthodoxy of multiculturalism (E) and declares that little of the new orthodoxy of multiculturalism exists (A). Against the editor's position, the passage declares that Aristotle, Augustine, and Milton are alive and well in the academy (B); that a charge of intellectual obscenity will pack the house (C); and that juicy attacks by the multiculturalists have gotten students to read books (D).

14. **(A)** The passage notes that Pound is often seen as an anti-Semite. It does not assert, however, that Pound *was* an anti-Semite (A). The passage also notes that Pound is often seen as a fascist (C), or a literary genius (B), and that critics often find themselves framed by a kind of critical Cold War (D), and often resemble the role of Marc Antony at the funeral in *Julius Caesar* (E).

15. **(D)** The passage concludes that legal assistant trainees should have internships (D). One premise is that internships are historically common (B), with apprenticeships (which are treated as kinds of internships (E)) dating back to 2100 B.C. in the Code of Hammurabi (C). Another premise is that physicians' training includes a formal one-year internship after graduation (A).

16. **(E)** This argument's *conclusion* is that textbooks deserve the considerable attention they have been getting (E). The premises are that textbooks are packed curricula (A) which are the essential source of information for students (B) and teachers (C) in elementary school, and that they outweigh all other sources in determining the day-to-day teaching in classrooms (D).

17. **(A)** This passage argues that visual form is important to network television newscasts just as the verbal content of the story. If visual form were not as important (A), this would weaken the argument. The passage claims that the visual form's importance is due in part to the fact that it conveys the aesthetic value of visual content (B). If this is true, it would strengthen the argument. It is irrelevant to the importance of visual form whether or not network news stories have remained static over the past 30 years (C), whether the three networks tend to select similar stories (D), and whether there has been as much analysis of visual form as of verbal content (E).

18. **(E)** This argument concludes that people are as interested in the Bible today as they were before (E). This contradicts the assertion that the less media-saturated generations of long ago had a greater hunger for the "Word" than the modern world (C). As one premise, the argument states that there has been an explosion of translations of the Bible in recent years (A). The argument does not claim that we *should* multiply the amount of labor over one translation by the number of new translations (D), although it does claim that if we do, we will understand the premise that the production of new translations of the Bible is an awesome task (B).

19. **(B)** The original argument moves from the fact that the two neighboring houses are similar in some characteristics (age and builder) to the claim that one further characteristic which one of them has (needing new siding) will be shared by the other. Clearly the builder and the siding's age are relevant to the state of the siding, so this argument has some initial plausibility. However, if the two houses differ in the highly relevant area of the material of the siding, as (B) proposes, much of that plausibility would disappear. Answers (A) and (C) do not address the similarities between the two houses and so have little to do with this argument. Nor with its conclusion — the siding may need replacing regardless of what the guarantee says or whether the owner can afford the repair. (D) does compare the two houses and notes a difference between them, but the skills of the owner are not obviously relevant to the issue of whether the siding will wear out at the same time. (E), on the other hand, finds a relevant similarity between the two houses, so would strengthen the argument rather than weaken it.

---

20. **(C)** The basic argument moves from the claim that each member (thing) of the whole (universe) has a certain property (began in time) to the claim that the whole has that property, the pattern described in (C). This is an inherently unreliable argument pattern, as knows anyone who has ever made a terrible-tasting mess by mixing together good-tasting things. This is not quite the same argument as that objected to in (A), for the original argument does not claim that everything began at the same time, though it does start by claiming that each thing began at some time. The objection in (B) also does not apply, since questions of causation are beyond the scope of the argument. Nor is (D) relevant, since the original argument does not compare the things in the universe and the universe as a whole for any other property than having a beginning. So it does not move from one such comparison to another. Finally, (E) does not apply, since it would not be illogical for the universe both to be the longest-lasting thing *and* to have had a beginning.

---

21. **(D)** There are two unspoken assumptions in the passage. The first occurs when the author interprets the mother's remark to mean "Buckle your seat belt." As the next sentence in the passage indicates, if the remark did not mean "Buckle your seat belt," it would be irrelevant to the daughter's situation. Obviously, the author assumes that the mother's remark is relevant, which corresponds to answer (D). The second assumption is that the daughter will be uninterested in irrelevant comments. The answer cannot be (B), since it contradicts the second assumption. (A) is out since the passage says that the daughter is uninterested only for the moment in what wise drivers do. It may be reasonable to think that the mother wants her daughter to fasten her seat belt, but this does not clearly assume that teenagers generally do not use seat belts or even that this girl does not. So (E) is not necessarily assumed. Nor is (C), since the reason that the mother wants her daughter to fasten her seat belt is not given. It may be out of concern for the law or insurance rates, as much as for danger.

22. **(D)** This study only examines the relationship between using steroids and having a certain level of high-density lipoproteins in the blood. It found a regular pattern of lower levels with steroid users than with similar non-users and also a pattern of lower levels with higher steroid use. Both of these offer good support for the claim that steroid use causes the lower levels of lipoproteins, answer (D). The study did not look directly at the relationship between steroid use and heart attacks; this connection can only be made by bringing in the additional information — from some other source — about the connection between lipoprotein levels and heart attacks. Thus, both (B) and (C) go beyond this study. (A) goes against the study, for all of the subjects of the study were body-builders, yet only steroid users seem to have been affected. The same comment applies to (E), though it is more precise about the effect involved.

23. **(C)** Dr. Spock is presented as an expert in the care of small children ("famous baby doctor") and, by context, at least, not an expert in the world economy. However, the fact that he is not an expert does not mean that his views are wrong and, so, to be rejected. He may very well be right and even have good evidence for his views, even though he is not an expert. So, (A) and (D) are not the proper responses. Nor is (B), for he is not an expert on world economy but on

child-rearing, so — as the first sentence says — his views on the former subject carry no special weight. That leaves him in the position of everyone else; his views must be evaluated on their own merit, without reference to his expertise in this or some other area. Finally, even if Dr. Spock were an expert in the world economy, it does not follow that his view is to be accepted, for experts can disagree and are sometimes demonstrably wrong. The usual procedures for evaluation are just somewhat different for experts, but the advice in (C) still applies.

---

24. **(D)** The logically crucial features of Einstein's case is that he predicted a phenomenon before it was observed and that the standard theory of the time said the prediction was wrong. Both of these features recur in Halley's case, though in slightly different form (the standard theory did not say that the comet would not appear on Halley's schedule, but only that it was impossible to predict the appearance of the comets). Neither Copernicus (A) nor Kepler (B) predicted phenomena before they were observed, they merely accounted for the observed phenomena by theories different from the standard theory (and, in Kepler's case, more simply than the standard theory). Galileo (C) observed a phenomenon that the standard theory denied, but did not predict it before he observed it (nor did it follow from the theory he was using). Herschel (E) observed a phenomenon predicted by the standard theory, not one contrary to it.

Section 5 –
Writing Sample

Baldwin State University is seeking a teacher-scholar who will help enhance the image of the university and help prove that we are more than just a state college accepting local high school graduates. A major part of realizing this goal will be recruiting skilled, teaching and student oriented faculty. While the university has made it clear that it expects its faculty to make research contributions, it is also clear that the university views teaching as its highest academic priority.

What we are essentially faced with is making a decision about the Mathematics Department's academic priorities. Do we value teaching most highly or research mostly highly? If we are going to place emphasis on teaching, then Mr. Smith is clearly the better choice. On the other hand, should we choose to stress research, I suspect that we would be better off appointing Ms. Jones.

I believe that the university has given priority to its teaching mission and must therefore recommend that the department appoint Mr. Smith to the tenure-track position of assistant professor.

Smith is clearly better suited to making teaching his first priority. He has three years of full-time experience at the University of West Virginia and I note that his student teaching evaluations are excellent. Moreover, his friendly, relaxed style will be an asset in retaining students as will his desire to spend as much time as necessary with students, even if this time is beyond his required office hours.

Certainly, another of the strong points of his candidacy is the fact that Smith has academic preparation in fields besides mathematics. His economics background is especially useful in allowing him to demonstrate practical applications of classroom lessons.

Though Smith's research background is slightly shaky, it should be kept in mind at all times that his principal responsibility while on faculty will be teaching, a task at which he clearly excels. It should also be remembered that he has published two papers in respected journals and is coauthoring a statistics textbook.

Ms. Jones' academic credentials are indisputably outstanding and her research background is rather strong, especially for her age. She has coauthored three textbooks and is working on a book of her own. In this position, however, the emphasis would be on teaching rather than research. The bulk of her time would be spent interacting with students.

While Ms. Jones has excellent research potential, I think it only honest to say that her teaching skills are weak. Her student evaluations have consistently been poor (a 2.85 is less than the mediocre midpoint of a 1-to-5 scale) and suggest that there is a problem with her teaching rather than the attitude of her students. Her unwillingness to spend extra time with students is a critical flaw in the CHARACTER of any university faculty member and cannot be remedied by a teaching skills improvement seminar.

While she may be a talented researcher, Ms. Jones is clearly a mediocre teacher at best. This shortcoming automatically disqualifies her from further consideration for the position, as teaching would be a major portion of the responsibilities of this position.

I strongly recommend John Smith for the position. He has an excellent rapport with students and is a dedicated teacher. Furthermore, he is a knowledgeable scholar and has published serious works in noteworthy journals. His diverse educational background is also a major asset as it gives the university some flexibility in terms of his teaching assignments. It should also be kept in mind that his attendance at state universities would most likely give him a better understanding of the average student we normally enroll at Baldwin State University.

Essay Explanation

This essay is well written because it follows the basic guidelines of good writing. The situation is clearly presented in the opening paragraphs along with the author's position. Both the problem and the author's position are clearly and effectively stated; there is no ambiguity.

Varying sentence lengths and varying sentence structures are used in the essay to avoid the impression that the essay "drones" monotonously. This is more important than you might think. Style definitely counts in the grading of LSAT writing samples by individual law schools.

The essay discusses the strengths and weaknesses of both candidates in relation to the two criteria for appointment to the position. In supporting a position, relevant information regarding both candidates is presented.

Opposing points are brought up and dealt with. In order for an essay to be credible, it must show that opposing viewpoints have been considered and outweighed. A one-sided essay is not effective.

Grammar, vocabulary and punctuation are all very important. Even the most well written essay can be destroyed if sloppy grammar, mispunctuation and spelling errors give the impression that the author is stupid.

Attacking the Reading Comprehension Questions

The Reading Comprehension questions measure your ability to read a selection, to reason, and to comprehend complex, lengthy passages similar to the readings in law school assignments.

It is crucial to note that you are to answer questions based upon the information in the passage. You are not to answer questions based upon information you have gathered outside of the test itself.

Important Information!

You will be presented with reading passages about 450-words in length followed by five to eight questions. **The subjects of the passages cover a variety of topics.** Some of the articles may interest you and relate to a subject with which you have some familiarity; other passages may neither interest you nor relate to an area with which you have a great deal of prior knowledge. The topics of the passages may include law, the humanities, natural sciences, and social sciences. The category of humanities can include theater, literature, architecture, art, music, and philosophy. Passages may cover topics such as the films of Alfred Hitchcock, the writing of Sherwood Anderson, the design of Gothic architecture, the use of collage as an art medium, jazz as a means of musical expression, and the comparisons and contrasts of deductive and inductive thinking. The category of natural sciences can include chemistry, geology, physics, and astronomy. A natural science reading passage on the Law School Admission Test, then, might include information on consumer chemistry, photosynthesis, sedimentary rocks, friction, and galaxies. The social sciences typically include anthropology, psychology, history, sociology, and archaeology. Reading passages may cover such topics as Cro-Magnon discoveries, behaviorism, the causes of the American Revolutionary War, the caste system, and Pompeii. Since so many disciplines appear on the LSAT, it is likely that at least some of the material will be unfamiliar to you.

On Target!

Regardless of the subject of the passage, every Reading Comprehension questions that you will encounter on the LSAT will be able to fall into one of six types. We will teach you these six types of questions and how to attack them.

In this section, you'll learn how to:

- **Identify the six different types of reading questions.**

- **Read the passages to best answer the questions.**

- **Read the questions to get the correct answers faster and more consistently.**

About the Directions

> <u>DIRECTIONS</u>: Read each passage and answer the questions that follow. Each question will be based on the information stated or implied in the passage or its introduction.

There are two points about the directions that we'd like to make. First, you must answer questions based upon what is stated or implied in the passage. As we mentioned before, these questions are not meant to test knowledge that you have acquired outside of the test itself. Answering questions based upon your outside knowledge can quickly lead to incorrect answers. Only answer the questions based on what you read in the passage.

Second, you are to choose the best answer for each question. It may be that none of the answers provided are overly impressive. Nonetheless, it is your job to choose the best answer from the possible choices.

Additionally, if you must choose the best answer provided, it is necessary that you read all of the answer choices. Choice (A) may be a good answer, but it will not be the correct answer if choice (E) is better. This is extremely important: When answering a Reading Comprehension question, always read and consider every answer choice. There are no exceptions to this rule.

Important Information!

About the Reading Comprehension Questions

There are six types of Reading Comprehension questions:

*Important
Information!*

TYPES OF QUESTIONS

- **Main Idea**

- **Specific Detail**

- **Implied Idea**

- **Logical Structure**

- **Further Application**

- **Tone**

We will now discuss each of these question types.

Question Type 1: MAIN IDEA QUESTIONS

*Important
Information!*

Main idea questions are extremely common on the LSAT. Often, the first question after the passage is a main idea question. Also, other questions may be directly or indirectly based upon the main idea of the passage.

Main idea questions are usually worded three ways:

a. **The main idea of the passage is . . .**

b. **The primary purpose of the passage is . . .**

c. **The best title of the passage is . . .**

Main idea questions can be worded in other ways, but the three just mentioned are the most common.

What are the LSAT writers looking for as an answer to a main idea question? **The correct answer to a main idea question is considered by the writer to be the answer choice that most accurately describes what the author wrote about in the passage.** Here's an example of how to determine the main idea of a passage:

Important Information!

Let's assume we have a reading comprehension passage. Each paragraph of that passage discusses the economic, social, and foreign policies of one of the following presidents: Truman, Eisenhower, Kennedy, Johnson, Nixon, Ford, Carter, Reagan, Bush, and Clinton.

Let's assume that question number one asks for the best title of the passage. Choice (A) for this question is, "A Discussion of the Economic, Social, and Foreign Policies of the Presidents of the United States."

Setting aside for a moment the requirement that you always read all of the answer choices to a reading comprehension problem, do you think choice (A) is likely to be the correct answer or do you think choice (A) is likely to be incorrect? Take a moment and think about the question before going on.

You probably surmised that choice (A) is not likely to be correct. By using the phrase "of the Presidents," choice (A) implies a discussion of all of the presidents. The passage, however, only discusses presidents in the post-World War II era. Thus, choice (A) is probably too broad in its scope to be the correct answer.

Suppose choice (B) states, "A Comparison of the Social Policies of Presidents Nixon and Clinton." Because of the narrowness of this answer choice, it is also unlikely to be the correct answer.

From just these two example answer choices, we can see that correct answer choices to main idea questions are those answer choices that correctly describe the subject matter discussed in the passage.

Although the main idea of the passage can best be found by considering all of the passage, if the author is going to sum up the main idea in one or two sentences, those sentences are likely to be in the first or last paragraphs. **Try not to look beyond the first or last paragraph for the main idea.** It is often dangerous to look for the answer to a main idea question in the body of the passage. This is true because, very often, incorrect answers to main idea questions will be facts stated in the body of the passage. The LSAT writers place these facts as incorrect answer choices as traps. These facts are usually too narrow in scope to be the correct answer to a main idea question. Unfortunately, under the time pressures of the test, such answers appear to be correct because of their truthfulness. Because of this, the test writers tend to go out of their way to give you an answer choice that corresponds almost word for word with a portion of the passage.

Also, truthfulness is not the sole component of a correct answer to a main idea question. **Correct answers to main idea questions proportionally represent how time was spent in the passage.** Facts gleaned from the body of the passage are unlikely to do so, and, thus, despite their **attractiveness**, are likely to be incorrect.

At this point, we will look at a typical reading comprehension passage so that you can more clearly see what we are discussing and how it applies to the LSAT Reading Comprehension questions.

Bust it!

PASSAGE

The words "organic," "chemical," "natural," and "health" are among the most misunderstood, misused, and maligned in our vocabulary, especially when they are applied to our food.

All organic materials are complex combinations of chemicals and contain one chemical element in common—carbon. But not all chemicals occur in the form of organic material. All of our food supply is in organic form because it has come from animal or plant sources. Most man-made foods are also in organic form.

Today, our chief concern about things organic and chemical relates to how foods are grown and processed. Our greatest concern is about the substances used in growing and processing our food.

Organic fertilizers used in growing the plants we eat directly, or which are fed to the animals that furnish our meat, are all made by the living cells in animal or plant tissues. They contain nutrients such as nitrogen, phosphorus, potassium, sulfur, magnesium, and other essential minerals in complex combinations with carbon, hydrogen, and usually oxygen.

Inorganic or commercial fertilizers contain the same chemical nutrients, but in simpler forms, and not always in combination with carbon. It is inaccurate to refer to inorganic fertilizers as "artificial" just because they have not been made from living cells.

Bust it!

A plant is unaware of the type of fertilizer—organic or inorganic—that is furnishing the chemicals for its growth. It does demand that these building blocks be in inorganic form. Plant cells synthesize the complex materials needed for growth rather than absorbing them ready-made from the soil.

Organically-raised animals are fed on organically grown grasses and feed. They are not given growth hormones, antibiotics, or synthetic materials. But it is unlikely that an animal's cells are aware of whether the many essentials for their growth are being furnished by feed in the organic or inorganic form.

Bust it!

The primary purpose of the passage is to

(A)   analyze a frequent source of disagreement.
(B)   define terms.
(C)   explain a theory.
(D)   eliminate a misunderstanding by defining.
(E)   explore the implications of a finding.

The correct answer to the question is choice (D). Choice (D), however, is by no means a perfect answer choice. It is correct because it is less flawed than the other choices.

Choice (A) is incorrect because we don't know of any disagreement and we don't know that this disagreement arises frequently. You could only have selected choice (A) had you made certain assumptions based on the passage. Making assumptions of this nature is likely to lead to incorrect answers on main idea questions. Again, we want to emphasize that you should answer the question based on information given in the passages, not on outside knowledge.

Choice (B) is incorrect because it is too narrow in its scope. The author does more than simply define terms. He or she uses those definitions to make points and reach conclusions. Choice (C) is incorrect because the passage does not explain a theory. Choice (E) is incorrect for at least two reasons. First, there is no "finding" in the passage. Second, even if one could find evidence of "finding" in this passage, there is still no exploration of such a finding.

This brings us to choice (D). Choice (D) is correct because the purpose of the passage is to eliminate a misunderstanding. We know that the author is concerned with misunderstandings because he or she sets this forth in the first paragraph. We also know that the author makes frequent use of definitions in the paragraph. Hence, choice (D) is the best. (NOTE: The information provided in the first paragraph was useful in arriving at the correct answer.)

Bust it!

To be honest, however, we must admit that choice (D) is by no stretch of the imagination a great answer choice. The flaws in choice (D), however, are not so much caused by the answer choice itself as they are caused by the rambling nature of the passage.

The passage begins by telling us that certain words are "misunderstood, misused, and maligned in our vocabulary." Without telling us how these words have been misunderstood or misused, the passage then launches into a rather abbreviated and elementary discussion of organic chemistry and some of its applications. The passage concludes by telling us "it is unlikely that an animal's cells are aware of whether the many essentials for their growth are being furnished by feed in the organic or inorganic form."

Bust it!

The problem with choice (D) is that, because we have never been precisely told in what manner certain words have been "misunderstood, misused, or maligned," it is extremely difficult for us to know whether this "misunderstanding" has been "eliminated."

That being said, choice (D) is, nevertheless, the best of the lot because it is clear that the passage spends much of its time defining terms and that the author is concerned with misunderstandings.

As mentioned before, we are not so much concerned with finding a great answer, or a perfect answer, as we are with finding the best answer.

The techniques of working from the answer choices is of paramount importance in answering Reading Comprehension problems. You must work from the answer choices; there is no other way. To attempt to formulate your own answer to a Reading Comprehension question would only waste time.

Eliminating Answer Choices

Similarly, when answering Reading Comprehension problems, **you must use the process of elimination.** By the process of elimination we mean that, in the problem above, choice (D) must be the best answer because it is less flawed than choices (A), (B), (C), or (E). With all reading comprehension questions, you could always create a "better" answer. But you are to choose the best from the answer choices that have been provided, and that implies eliminating the rest of the answer choices.

Question Type 2: SPECIFIC DETAIL QUESTIONS

Specific detail questions, as the name implies, ask questions based upon narrow points found in the passage. Specific detail questions will often be introduced with language similar to the following:

Look!

Important Strategy

> **a. According to the passage, ...**
>
> **b. Which of the following is stated in the passage?**

To answer a specific detail question, read the question and go through the answer choices, eliminating any that are clearly incorrect. This technique utilizes the process of elimination. This initial pass through the answer choices should eliminate two or three answer choices.

Once you've eliminated the obvious wrong choices, it is usually necessary to go back to the line or lines of the passage giving rise to the question. For this reason, **it is always a good idea to pay attention to paragraphs with important points in the passage and note the function of those paragraphs within the passage. This will decrease the amount of time it takes you to find these paragraphs when answering specific detail questions.**

Do not attempt to complete a specific detail question without going back to the passage. The passages are much too dense, and the remaining two or three answer choices are always close in terms of their relative correctness. After having gone back to the passage, return to the answer choices, eliminate one or two answer choices, and choose the best answer choice.

Important Information!

If you are still not sure which is the correct answer choice, do not go back to the passage another time. You will only waste time by doing so. If you have eliminated one or more of the answer choices, even if you are not certain which of the remaining choices is correct, choose the answer choice you think is the best and go on to the next question.

Here's an example using the same passage used for main idea questions:

EXAMPLE

According to the passage, nearly all of man's food supply

    (A)   **has been organically processed.**
    (B)   **has been organically grown.**
    (C)   **is both organic and inorganic because it comes from both plants and animals.**
    (D)   **has been contaminated by artificial additives.**
    (E)   **is in organic form because it is the product of living cells.**

Bust it!

While answering this question, your thought processes may run along the following lines: Choice (A) is probably not correct because the idea of organic processing seems to be a contradiction in terms. Choice (B) seems better than choice (A), but much of man's food supply comes from animals and fish, and we don't usually speak in terms of animals being grown. We grow plants, but we raise animals.

Choice (C) seems wrong because it implies that either plants or animals is an inorganic source. Choice (D) seems too strong to be correct and is not supported by the passage. Choice (E) seems good because we remember some tie-in between organic things being products of living cells.

At this point, however, it would not be wise to answer the question without going back to the passage. Having seen the answer choices once, you are now in a good position to return to the passage.

Skimming quickly through the passage and remembering where important points were made, we come across the words "food supply" in the third sentence of the second paragraph. We are told that "all of our food supply is in organic form because it has come from animal or plant sources."

Returning again to the answer choices, we can now quickly toss out choices (A), (B), and (D) because the paragraph concerning the food supply has nothing to do with how things are processed or grown. Nor does that paragraph deal with artificial additives.

Bust it!

Choices (C) and (E) remain. Choice (C), although seemingly incorrect at first glance, is very tempting (as the second best answer choice usually is), but it must be eliminated because it says that man's food supply is "both organic and inorganic." When you returned to the passage, you found that it clearly states, "all of our food supply is in organic form." If all of the food supply is organic, then none of it is inorganic, so we must eliminate choice (C).

This leaves choice (E), which is the correct answer. Note that choice (E) states, "is in organic form because it is the product of living cells." The paragraph states that "our food supply is in organic form because it has come from animal or plant sources." Note that the phrases "is the product of living cells" and "has come from animal or plant sources" are not identical.

Whether these two phrases are close enough in meaning to make this a great answer choice will cast a certain level of doubt upon choice (E). But, as we have stated before, even though we cannot be absolutely sure that choice (E) is not flawed, it is not as clearly flawed as choice (C), which incorrectly proclaims that man's food supply is partially inorganic. Thus, by working closely with the answer choices and using the process of elimination, we see that we must select choice (E) as the best answer choice for the question.

Bust it!

There is a variation on the specific detail question which comes up with sufficient regularity on the LSAT. Consider this question based on the same passage:

> **The passage contains information that would answer all of the following questions EXCEPT:**
>
> (A)   **Why is organic fertilizer superior to inorganic fertilizer?**
> (B)   **What are organic materials?**
> (C)   **Do plants require nutrients in organic or inorganic form?**
> (D)   **What is the common chemical in all organic materials?**
> (E)   **Why is it inaccurate to call inorganic fertilizers "artificial"?**

We will call this type of problem a reverse specific detail problem. Instead of asking which is a specific detail of the problem, this type of problem asks which is not a specific detail.

Bust it!

The best answer is choice (A). We are not given any information that helps us know why organic fertilizer is superior to inorganic fertilizer. To the contrary, the first sentence of paragraph four indicates that organic fertilizer is not superior.

Remembering the key points in the passage will help you eliminate some of these choices without second thought. But some of the choices may seem correct. To eliminate all the incorrect answer choices you must go back to the passage and look for specific sentences that will answer the questions posed in the answer choices:

　　　　The first sentence of the second paragraph provides information that would help us answer the question posed in choice (B). The second sentence of the sixth paragraph helps us to answer the question found in choice (C). That sentence says a plant demands that these building blocks be in inorganic form. "These" refers to the chemicals needed for growth, noted in the previous sentence. And the chemicals, listed at the end of the fourth paragraph, are also termed "nutrients." The first sentence of the second paragraph tells us that carbon is the common chemical in all organic materials, thus answering choice (D). And the second sentence of the fifth paragraph tells us why it is inaccurate to call inorganic fertilizers "artificial," thus eliminating choice (E).

　　　　As you can see, the reverse specific detail type of questions can cause you to waste an excessive amount of time. To find the information necessary to eliminate the incorrect choices, you had to return to the second, fourth, fifth, and sixth paragraphs. **If all questions on the LSAT are of equal value, why return to the passage four times so that you can get one question correct?** It isn't a very good time-saving strategy. We, therefore, recommend the following procedures for reverse specific detail questions:

　　　　Upon spotting a reverse specific detail question, read all of the answer choices and eliminate any that you know are not the correct answer choice. (Do not go back to the passage to perform this operation.) If you can eliminate two or three of the answer choices, make your best guess at the correct answer. This will save you a lot of time. Only if you cannot eliminate at least two of the answer choices should you return to the passage to look for information to eliminate answer choices. Even then, only return to the passage once. Use the information you found in the passage to eliminate any incorrect answer choices and then make your best guess from the remaining answers.

Question Type 3: IMPLIED IDEA QUESTIONS

Implied idea questions test your ability to recognize information that is not explicitly stated in the passage, but is strongly implied. Such questions can refer to specific details or more general ideas and are usually worded in one of the following ways:

*Important
Information!*

> a. It can be inferred . . .
>
> b. The passage suggests . . .
>
> c. The author probably considers . . .
>
> d. The author implies that . . .

To answer an implied idea question, read the question and the answer choices, eliminating the two or three weaker answer choices. Read the section of the passage that contains the details needed to answer the question again. Remember where to look in the passage by paying attention to the important paragraphs as you read the passage. Select the best answer.

Avoid the temptation to make unwarranted assumptions. The majority of wrong answer choices in implied idea questions try to draw you into making assumptions for which you do not have sufficient facts. Be careful of your assumptions. Avoid using your outside knowledge. Use only the information in the passage.

Here's an example using the organic fertilizer passage previously presented:

EXAMPLE

It can be inferred from the passage that

(A) animals must convert synthetic fertilizers to organic form to benefit from them.

(B) organically raised animals are more likely to be disease-free than those raised inorganically.

(C) organically raised animals process chemical nutrients in the same way as organically raised plants.

(D) organically raised animals tend to be smaller than animals raised inorganically.

(E) animals can use chemical nutrients for growth in either organic or inorganic form.

Upon our first pass through the answer choices, we can eliminate choices (B), (C), and (D). Choice (B) is not correct because there is no mention whatsoever of which type of feeding is likely to produce disease-free animals. We are told that organically fed animals are not given antibiotics, but cannot draw any conclusions concerning the likelihood of disease from a barren statement about antibiotics. Choice (C) is not correct because there is nothing in the passage that would lead us to believe that animals process nutrients in the same way that plants do. And, in choice (D), there is no mention in the passage that the type of feeding can affect the size of the animal.

Bust it!

We are now down to choices (A) and (E). Remembering that the last paragraph dealt with animals, we return to that paragraph. The last sentence tells us it is unlikely that an animal's cells are aware of whether the nutrients are furnished in organic or inorganic form.

Bust it!

If the animal's cells are likely to be unaware of the form of the nutrients, then it is not likely that synthetic fertilizers must be converted to organic form. Thus, we eliminate choice (A).

Additionally, if the animal's cells are unaware of the form of the nutrients, then it is likely, as stated in choice (E), that animals can use nutrients for growth in either organic or inorganic form. Choice (E) is correct.

Question Type 4: LOGICAL STRUCTURE QUESTIONS

Important Information!

Logical structure questions test your ability to analyze the organization of the author's argument. These questions focus on the organization of the passage as a whole, the organization of a paragraph, or the role of a particular detail in the structure of the argument.

If a logical structure question concerns the entire passage, the key to answering the question is to select the answer choice that fully and precisely describes the structure of the passage. **Therefore, some logical structure questions are similar to main idea questions. You must search for an answer choice that is neither too broad nor too narrow.**

If a logical structure question concerns either a paragraph or a section of a paragraph, your focus must be more narrow. You must ask yourself one of two questions. First, what is the function of this paragraph within the passage? To answer this question, it may be helpful to get an idea of the purpose of the other paragraphs of the passage. Again, you should be paying attention to key paragraphs and their function in the structure of the passage as you read it.

Second, what is the function of this sentence within the paragraph? To answer this question, it is a good idea to keep in mind the function of the paragraph housing the sentence in question. **The sentence in question will usually do one of three things. It will support the main idea, contradict the main idea, or serve as a stepping-stone to ideas conveyed in the next paragraph.**

Very often, logical structure questions concerning paragraphs or specific sentences will make specific references to those paragraphs or sentences. An example of such a question might be, "the author cites Newton (line 34) because . . ."

If confronted with such a question, line 34 must be the place you begin your inquiry. You should, however, remember to ask yourself what the purpose of the paragraph which contains line 34 is.

Additionally, simply because you are referred to line 34 does not automatically mean the answer to the question will be found in line 34 or even in the paragraph containing line 34. **When a question refers to a line in the passage, that line is the beginning of your inquiry. Realize, however, that you may well have to go very far from that line to discover the correct answer. This is a trap placed by the LSAT writers to make you waste time.**

Because of the possibility of wasting time when faced with a logical structure question (as with all Reading Comprehension questions), you should eliminate as many answer choices as you can before going back to the passage. Once you've eliminated at least two answer choices, go back to the passage and find information to

Important Information!

Important Strategy

eliminate the other choices. Don't spend too much time, and only go back to the passage once. When you cannot eliminate any more choices, make your best guess at the correct answer and move on.

Here's an example of a logical structure question based on the same passage we've been using for other examples:

EXAMPLE

Which of the following statements best describes the organization of the passage?

(A)   A dispute is presented and resolved.

(B)   A problem is outlined and a solution is proposed.

(C)   A misunderstanding is underscored and clarifying definitions are presented.

(D)   A critique is made and supporting evidence is presented.

(E)   A current hypothesis is examined and an alternative is suggested.

Bust it!

Note that, in terms of scope, this question is similar to a main idea question. Both questions look at the entire passage. To answer this question, we must work from the answer choices and use the process of elimination.

Choice (A) appears weak because there is neither a dispute nor a resolution of a dispute.

Choice (B) is weak for a similar reason. We don't really have a problem. Even if we stretch the definition of a "problem" (and it is always a bad idea to stretch the definition of a word on the LSAT) to

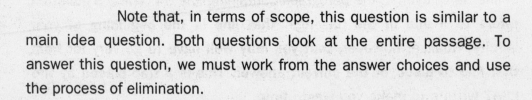

include the population's misuse of certain words (organic, chemical), we still do not have a solution to that problem. That the people who read this passage might not misuse the relevant words does not mean the problem has been cleared up for the general population.

Upon initial consideration, choice (C) looks decent. The first paragraph does mention a misunderstanding, and the rest of the passage does contain numerous definitions.

Bust it!

Choice (D) is weak because we have neither a critique nor supporting evidence.

Choice (E) is also incorrect. We do not have a hypothesis, nor do we have an alternative.

Having read all of the possible answers, choice (C) is the correct answer. Once again, note that the correct answer tied into the main idea: the logical structure of the passage was related to the main idea.

Question Type 5: FURTHER APPLICATION QUESTIONS

Further application questions require you to relate the ideas presented in the passage to a broader context or a context that is not the same as the one found in the passage. Further application questions take on forms similar to the following:

Important Information!

a.   The passage most likely appeared in a . . .

b.   The passage is most relevant to which field of study . . .

To answer a further application problem, keep in mind the main idea of the passage. It is also helpful to pay attention to how details have been used in the passage. Finally, look at the tone

Look!

*Important
Strategy*

the author used in the passage. Here's an example of a further application problem using the passage on organic fertilizer:

EXAMPLE

The passage most likely appeared in a(n)

(A)   nutrition textbook.
(B)   encyclopedia.
(C)   popular science magazine.
(D)   medical journal.
(E)   college chemistry textbook.

Once again, we must work from the answer choices and use the process of elimination. As to choice (A), a nutrition textbook would be designed to tell us what kinds of food to eat and why we should eat those foods. Some nutrition books might also discuss using vitamins. Much of our passage concerns the requirements for fertilizers or the types of fertilizers required by plant life. Such paragraphs are out of place in a nutrition book, making choice (A) inappropriate.

Bust it!

As to choice (B), the purpose of an encyclopedia is to give the reader straight forward information concerning a topic. An encyclopedia does not usually get involved in clearing up misunderstandings between different topics. Hence, choice (B) is incorrect.

Choice (D) is incorrect. Most articles in medical journals report the latest findings of scientific studies that might be helpful to the medical profession. For example, there might be a study on the rate of skin cancer of polar bears that were exposed to 16 hours of sun a day after having been given 200 grams of vitamin C a day. The language of the medical journal is likely to be much more technical than that of the passage. Most doctors would have learned the context of the passage in their science courses in college.

Choice (E) is incorrect because our passage is outside the scope of a chemistry textbook. Chemistry textbooks are concerned with the molecular or atomic make-up of cells and how certain cells interact with other cells. Chemistry textbooks spend a lot of time on formulas. Also, a chemistry textbook would present the information in a much more technical and complex language.

Bust it!

This leaves choice (C), which is the correct answer. The scope of a popular science magazine would be quite broad and, therefore, this passage is not outside the realm of a popular science magazine. Second, this passage (with its great reliance on definitions) has been written for a broad audience, all of whom may not be familiar with the subject matter. You should determine that the passage was written for a broad audience because of its simple language and lack of technical terminology. The audience of a popular science magazine is likely to be the average reader as well as scientists. Thus, choice (C) is correct.

Choice (C) is the correct answer, not because it is absolutely certain that the passage would appear in a popular science magazine, but because choice (C) is better than the rest of the answer choices. Once again, you must work from the answer choices given and use the process of elimination.

Question Type 6: TONE QUESTIONS

Tone questions test your ability to answer questions concerning the tone of the author. A tone question can be based on the entire passage, or just a part of a passage. **As you read passages, try to be sensitive to the tone of the author.**

Important Strategy

To answer tone questions of a general nature, you must first ask yourself whether the tone of the author is positive, negative, or neutral. **A positive tone would present support of a topic or action. A negative tone would present disapproval of a topic or action. A neutral tone would present both sides of a topic or action and neither support nor disapproval.** After answering this question, go through the answer choices. You will probably be able to eliminate two or three answer choices.

To work your way down to the correct answer choice, ask yourself to what degree the author is positive, negative, or neutral. Is the author extremely positive, or only slightly positive? Look at the remaining answer choices and think about the connotations and implications of the remaining answer choices. Tone questions rely to a certain degree upon your knowing the meanings of words. Select the answer choice that best reflects the author's tone and intensity.

Important Strategy

When answering a tone question which concerns the entire passage, it is usually a good idea not to go back to the passage. You do not have time to read the entire passage again and focusing on a portion of the passage could lead you astray.

If the tone question is only based on a portion of the passage, read the answer choices, eliminating any obviously incorrect answers. Then go back and read the relevant portion of the passage. After having read the relevant portion of the passage, try to judge the tone. Then eliminate any other choices that are incorrect. Next, try and identify the intensity of the author's tone. Is it very negative? Slightly negative? Once again, pay attention to the connotations of the words. Finally, select the best answer choice.

EXAMPLE

The author's attitude toward inorganic fertilizers can best be described as

(A) extremely biased.
(B) hostile.
(C) mildly critical.
(D) objective or neutral.
(E) enthusiastically supportive.

Bust it!

Because this is a tone question based on only part of the passage, you must first eliminate any obviously wrong choices. Once you've done that, go back to the passage and read the fifth paragraph of the passage again. The overall tone of the paragraph is somewhat neutral. The author is simply relating facts about inorganic fertilizers.

This eliminates choices (A), (B), and (E). These choices are much too intense to fit the paragraph. You can eliminate choice (C) because the second sentence of the paragraph is, if anything, defends the use of inorganic fertilizers. So, by the process of elimination, choice (D) is the correct answer.

Reading the Passages

The first point we wish to discuss concerns how you will use your time on the Reading Comprehension questions. It is clear that there are two tasks that must be performed during Reading Comprehension questions: First, you must read the passage. Second, you must answer the questions.

Look!

Important Strategy

Bust it!

How do you want to use the limited time you have for this section? Do you want to spend more time reading the passage than answering the questions? Should you spend more time answering the questions than reading the passage? Should you spend equal amounts of time on each?

As we showed you throughout our explanation of the types of Reading Comprehension questions you'll encounter on the LSAT, you should spend most of your time answering the questions. Spending most of the time answering the questions probably runs counter to what you would think is the preferred method. Let's examine the issue in greater detail:

You might think that a total understanding of the passage would make the questions very easy to answer. This assumption is wrong. Even if you had a perfect knowledge of the passage, the questions would still be difficult.

The difficulty arises because there will not be much difference between two or three of the answer choices presented. You should be able to eliminate at least two or three answer choices without going back to the passage. This leaves you with two or three choices to choose from. **A perfect understanding of the passage is not going to help you to notice the distinction between the shades of meaning of the two or three best answer choices remaining. To notice the difference between the remaining answer choices, you are going to need to go back to the passage.** If you know you will have to go back to the passage to find the best answer, why spend a lot of time trying to gain a perfect understanding of the passage? **Time spent carefully and completely reading the passage (this doesn't mean reading for perfect understanding) is time that you won't have to go back to the passage to consider and eliminate the second-best answer choices.**

Watching the Clock!

We don't mean to imply that you should ignore or disregard the passage. **We are only suggesting that you spend more time on the answer choices and less time actually reading the passage**. Keep in mind that you get credit for answering the questions, not for understanding the passage.

How then should you read the passage? **You should read the passage fairly quickly and without stopping.** This does not mean you should "speed read" the passage. Nor does it mean you should skip sentences or words. It means you should read through the passage at a decent pace, understanding it as best you can. Don't re-read complex sentences over and over until you understand them. Simply read them once, paying attention and gaining as much understanding as you can.

Watching the Clock!

What should you be trying to get out of the passage during your initial reading? We've pointed these items out in our discussion of the types of Reading Comprehension questions. Here are the three items your should be concerned with:

1. **The main idea of the passage**

2. **The organization of the passage**

3. **The tone the author uses in the passage**

Look!

Important Strategy

First of all, and most importantly, you should be trying to understand **the main idea of the passage**. The main idea will almost always be a topic of one of the questions you'll have to answer, and the main idea is the cornerstone upon which the rest of the passage is built. Keep in mind that in a passage of about 400 words, the main idea is likely to control most of the passage.

*Important
Strategy*

Second, you would like to formulate some idea as to **how the passage is organized**—the logical structure of the passage. Third, you want to pick up **the tone of the passage**. If you get these three things out of the passage, you will be in good shape to answer the questions.

Concerning the actual reading of the passage, we make one final point. Each time that you see a new paragraph, the author is probably introducing a new idea. Thus, whenever you see a new paragraph, you should ask yourself: what is the new idea introduced by this paragraph?

We don't expect you to be able to remember the new idea introduced by each new paragraph. But we do believe it would help if you are aware that a new idea is on the way.

To justify the manner in which we are suggesting you read the passage, we return to the various kinds of questions. If you recall, some of the questions force you to look at the "big picture": main idea questions or tone questions. Other questions focus in on part of passage: specific detail and implied Idea questions.

*Important
Strategy*

For "big picture" questions, a three-minute reading of the passage will usually suffice. Your task is not so much grasping the main idea, but determining which answer choices best express the main idea.

For more focused questions, you are going to have to return to the passage to answer the questions. **Why spend time attempting to memorize the details of the passage when you will refer back to those details to answer questions concerning those details? The most important thing is to have an idea of where those details are so that you can quickly find those details when needed.**

Reading the Questions

After you finish reading the passage, proceed immediately to the questions. Look at answer choice (A) in the first question and ask yourself whether you think it is a good choice, a bad choice, or whether you can't decide if it's a good or bad choice (neutral). Do the same with choices (B), (C), (D), and (E). During this first reading of the answer choices, you do not want to spend too much time with any one of the answer choices. You only want to get an idea whether each answer choice is in the ballpark or out of the ballpark.

Look!

Important Strategy

Additionally, at this time you want to avoid the temptation to compare any two of the answer choices. If choice (A) is decent and choice (B) is decent, there is a natural temptation to immediately want to decide between them. The problem with such a comparison at this stage of the game is that choice (E) may be clearly better than either choices (A) or (B). **Any effort spent comparing choices (A) and (B) would, therefore, clearly have been a waste of time.**

After the first reading of the answer choices, you should have been able to eliminate two or three answer choices. Focus very carefully on the remaining answer choices. It's now crunch time. Be careful of the language of these remaining answer choices. Try to be sensitive to the nuances of these answer choices.

If the type of question being asked is of a focused nature, now is the time to return to the appropriate section of the passage. **Do not attempt to answer a question of a focused nature without returning to the passage!** The passages are crammed with details. Relying on your memory for such details would be ill-advised.

*Important
Strategy*

Once you've read the pertinent section of the passage, return to the answer choices and read again the ones you haven't eliminated. Think about each answer choice for a few seconds and select the one you think is the best answer choice. **Do not return a second time to the passage for further information. Repeated trips to the passage for any given question will not serve to enlighten you. They will only waste time.**

Choosing the Best Answer Choice

It is an unfortunate truth that the line between the best and the second-best answer choice is a fine line indeed. Put another way, **the best answer choice is not always all that much better than the second-best answer choice.**

What are you to do, then, when you are not sure?

*Important
Strategy*

Before we answer that question, we feel it necessary to appropriately frame the question. By the very nature of the test, with regard to the verbal questions, even if you understand the question, you will not be absolutely certain of the correct answer in more than 80 percent of the questions.

The questions have been deliberately designed to leave you with a high degree of uncertainty at the moment you enter your selection. **The LSAT rewards people who can efficiently make decisions.** One of the reasons why the LSAT may have been designed this way is that a lawyer is faced with uncertainties during a trial. He or she often will probably have to make quick decisions during a trial that may affect the case and even the verdict. If someone has a hard time deciding on an answer for a LSAT question, he or she may have a hard time thinking quickly during a trial.

On all the sections of the LSAT, you must narrow down the answer choices as far as you can with any degree of certainty (usually there will be two, sometimes three, choices left), then pick the one you think is correct. **To spend so much time on each answer until you are certain you are correct is likely to create such serious time problems that you will do poorly on the test.**

You must narrow down the field, make your decision, and then go on to the next question. The more you practice making decisions within the time frame allotted by the test, the better you will do on the test.

Practicing for the Reading Comprehension Questions

One of the major problems you may have with Reading Comprehension questions is the passage itself. You may find the passage quite difficult. The reason for the difficulty is that the passage is usually outside the primary field of your study.

Look!

Important Strategy

For example, if you had majored in biology, you probably would have had an easier time reading a passage about genetics than if you had majored in music. **But, we'd like to reiterate, you are being** tested on your ability to understand information presented in the passage, not on your outside knowledge. If you find you are having trouble understanding the reading passages, you must hone your skill of reading and understanding unfamiliar material.

Important Strategy

Luckily, we have a suggestion that might help you to sharpen this skill and broaden your field of knowledge and interest: read the editorial column of a good daily newspaper. The editorial column may prove useful to you for a number of reasons.

First, newspaper editors tend to write on a wide range of topics. They write on music, art, foreign policy, Medicaid, taxes, sports, elections, economic policy, and the environment. The list goes on and on. Reading the editorial column of a good newspaper will help you to gain skills at reading in fields outside of your own.

Second, the editors tend to make their points in writings that are almost the same length as a LSAT passage: about 450 words. There are not too many places where writers develop ideas within a 450-word time frame. Reading the editorial column of a good newspaper will also help you become acclimated to reading passages where the theme is developed in a short space.

Important Strategy

If you are going to follow this suggestion, try to read the editorial without having read the title of the editorial. One of the reasons that Reading Comprehension passages are difficult is that they come without a title. The absence of a title places the burden on you of figuring out what the passage is all about, in effect, making you figure out the main idea.

Almost everything you read or see comes with a title: books, movies, newspaper articles, magazine articles. If you are reading it, it probably came with a title. Now look at a LSAT Reading Comprehension passage: no title. Thus, if you are going to read editorial columns, we recommend you try not to look at the title. Developing your ability to pick out the main idea of a writing when it has not been given to you is a skill that may come in handy on the LSAT.

Points to Remember

On Target!

✔   *Read the passage in no more than three minutes.*

✔   *While reading the passage, try to pick out the main idea, logical structure, and tone.*

✔   *Do not try to pick out or remember the details of the passage.*

✔   *Read the question, then read all of the answer choices. Eliminate the two or three mediocre answer choices.*

✔   *If the question concerns detailed information from the passage, return to the section of the passage where those details can be found.*

✔   *Read very carefully the remaining two or three answer choices. Pay attention to the nuances of each answer choice.*

✔   *Remember to answer Reading Comprehension questions based on the information provided in the passage. Do not base your answers upon prior knowledge.*

On Target!

✔   Do not make repeated trips to the passage to answer any one question.

✔   After you have given yourself an allotted amount of time to answer, select the answer you think is the best. Then go on to the next question.

✔   Memorize the directions for the Reading Comprehension questions before you take the test so that you don't waste time reading them while taking the actual LSAT.

Drill: Reading Comprehension

Line

(1)   Passion! What better word is there to describe opera? The vital core of opera is passion—sometimes violent, or joyful, loving, hateful, ecstatic, melancholic, vengeful; the gamut of
(5) emotions are exposed on the operatic stage and are transformed through the beauty of the music and the human voice. These emotions enter into an exalted state and, like everything else about opera, they are bigger than life. In opera, the ordinary
(10) becomes extraordinary.

Not only does passion reign on the operatic stage, but it also elicits as intense a response on the other side of the curtain. Opera audiences are known to erupt into wild outbursts—either giving
(15) performers wildly enthusiastic ovations and showering the stage with bouquets of flowers, or loudly hissing and booing and, even worse, throwing tomatoes and other "symbols of displeasure" onto the stage. Passion is returned
(20) with passion; indeed, the ardent devotion of some opera fans has stimulated the formation of cult-like groups around certain charismatic performers. It isn't difficult to understand how listeners can be awed by opera's grandeur and transported by the
(25) passions unfolding onstage.

Opera stands as one of the great cultural achievements of Western civilization. It represents a glorious fusion of the arts, combining drama, music, dance, and the visual arts. No one art form
(30) can be discounted; opera requires each of its components to fulfill its essential role—anything less, and the opera suffers. Perhaps no one understood this better than Richard Wagner, who insisted that he did not compose opera as such but,
(35) rather, created *Gesamtkunstwerk* ("Total-artwork"). He meant by this a synthesis of poetry, music, drama, and spectacle, in which each element cooperatively subordinates itself to the total purpose. That total purpose—the music-drama
(40) (opera)—is not a mere "entertainment" but a profound and compelling work of art that elevates the listeners and resonates with our humanity. Yet opera is pure artifice. If in the ordinary theater our disbelief must be willingly suspended in order to
(45) make the illusion of the play work, in opera that is no longer the question. We simply accept a world in which, among other things, people sing—

beautifully—whether of love, of death, or murder, or whatever. Thus, Samuel Johnson had a valid
(50) point in defining opera as "an irrational entertainment." The late Kenneth Clark, the eminent British art historian, once asked, "What on earth has given opera its prestige in Western civilization—a prestige that has outlasted so
(55) many different fashions and ways of thought?" He finds the answer in Dr. Johnson's definition: "…because it is irrational. 'What is too silly to be said may be sung'—well, yes; but what is too subtle to be said, or too deeply felt, or too
(60) revealing or too mysterious—these things can also be sung and only be sung."

Unusual for a rarefied pleasure (which it is often-times considered), opera today enjoys a flourishing and growing popularity. With the
(65) advent of modern technology, opera is able to reach millions of people around the world who would otherwise not be exposed to its splendor. The phonograph enabled opera to be brought into people's homes and, later, radio provided
(70) opera with a powerful and pervasive forum from which it attracted new listeners. More recently, the cinema and, especially, television have been instrumental in introducing opera to uninitiated audiences and converting many into fans.

1. The primary purpose of the passage is to

(A) compare the works of Wagner.
(B) describe the joy of opera.
(C) report on the resurgence of opera.
(D) critique the artificiality of opera.
(E) summarize a history of opera.

2. By calling opera *pure artifice*, the author in Line 43

(A) is attacking its value.
(B) recognizes the importance of *Gesamtkunstwerk*.
(C) agrees with the comment of Samuel Johnson.
(D) acknowledges its unrealistic character.
(E) is criticizing Wagner's operas.

3. From the passage, Clark's explanation for the longevity of opera

(A) relies precisely on its artificial nature.
(B) is based on the mutual passion created by audience and artists.
(C) is that it has adapted to technological changes.
(D) is derived from *Gesamtkunstwerk*.
(E) denies its irrationality.

4. The author argues wild outbursts of approval or symbols of displeasure by opera fans show

(A) the inconsistent quality of modern opera.
(B) the lack of sophistication of most audiences.
(C) audience indifference.
(D) the artificial nature of opera.
(E) the depth and breadth of emotional reactions.

5. Based on the information in the passage, one can conclude that

(A) a booming video market may put an end to opera attendance.
(B) television may bring opera to many homes.
(C) opera is an art form of the past.
(D) opera has never been popular but may become so in the future.
(E) opera was once popular but is no longer so.

6. Samuel Johnson's calling opera "irrational" shows

(A) his contempt for opera.
(B) the humor with which he viewed it.
(C) that it is an art form.
(D) that it is an easily comprehended art form.
(E) that it is not easily explained.

7. Opera enthusiasts

(A) merely accept the art form as it is.
(B) openly critique the form itself and try to change the form.
(C) hope to modify the art form through the years.
(D) themselves feel disdainful toward the fanciful world of opera.
(E) are few in numbers and will probably diminish with time.

8. The purpose of opera

(A) is primarily the presentation of the music.
(B) shows that music is secondary to the artwork itself.
(C) was not clearly understood by Wagner.
(D) requires that the disillusion of the viewer be kept alive.
(E) is outmoded in present-day society.

Line
(1)   The promise of finding long-term technological solutions to the problem of world food shortages seems difficult to fulfill. Many innovations that were once heavily supported and publicized, such *(5)* as fish-protein concentrate and protein from algae grown on petroleum substrates, have since fallen by the wayside. The proposals themselves were technically feasible, but they proved to be economically unviable and to yield food products *(10)* culturally unacceptable to their consumers. Recent innovations such as opaque-2 maize, Antarctic krill, and the wheat-rye hybrid triticale seem more promising, but it is too early to predict their ultimate fate. One characteristic common to *(15)* unsuccessful food innovations has been that, even with extensive government support, they often have not been technologically adapted or culturally acceptable to the people for whom they had been developed. A successful new technology, therefore, *(20)* must fit the entire sociocultural system in which it is to find a place. Security of crop yield, practicality of storage, palatability, and costs are much more significant than had previously been realized by the advocates of new technologies. For example, the *(25)* better protein quality in tortillas made from opaque-2 maize will be of only limited benefit to a family on the margin of subsistence if the new maize is not culturally acceptable or is more vulnerable to insects. The adoption of new food *(30)* technologies depends on more than these technical and cultural considerations; economic factors and governmental policies also strongly influence the ultimate success of any innovation. Economists in the Anglo-American tradition have taken the lead *(35)* in investigating the economics of technological innovation. Although they exaggerate in claiming that profitability is the key factor guiding technical change—they completely disregard the substantial effects of culture—they are correct in stressing the *(40)* importance of profits. Most technological innovations in agriculture can be fully used only by large landowners and are only adopted if these profit-oriented businesspeople believe that the innovation will increase their incomes. Thus,

(45)   innovations that carry high rewards for big
agribusiness groups will be adopted even if they
harm segments of the population and reduce the
availability of food in a country. Further, should
a new technology promise to alter substantially
(50)   the profits and losses associated with any
production system, those with economic power
will strive to maintain and improve their own
positions. Since large segments of the
populations of many developing countries are
(55)   close to the subsistence margin and essentially
powerless, they tend to be the losers in this
system unless they are aided by a government
policy that takes into account the needs of all
sectors of the economy. Therefore, although
(60)   technical advances in food production and
processing will perhaps be needed to ensure
food availability, meeting food needs will depend
much more on equalizing economic power
among the various segments of the populations
(65)   within the developing countries themselves.

9. With which one of the following statements
would the author most likely agree?

(A) Agribusiness groups have consistently
opposed technological innovations.
(B) Agribusiness groups act chiefly out of
economic self-interest.
(C) Agribusiness groups have been
misunderstood by Anglo-American
economists.
(D) Agribusiness groups nearly always welcome
technological innovations.
(E) The economic success of agribusiness
groups in developing countries will
automatically improve living conditions for
all people in those countries.

10. Which one of the following statements best
summarizes the author's evaluation of the
importance of technological advances in solving
the problem of world food shortages?

(A) They will succeed only if all people are given
adequate technological education.
(B) They remain the single greatest hope in
solving the problem of world food shortages.
(C) They are ultimately less important than
economic reforms in developing nations.
(D) They will succeed only if the governments of
developing countries support them.
(E) They will succeed only if they receive
widespread acceptance among powerful
agribusiness groups.

11. According to the passage, some past
technological food innovations, such as
protein from algae grown on petroleum
substrates, have failed because

(A) they were not technologically feasible.
(B) they did not receive adequate
government support.
(C) local producers did not understand the
new technology.
(D) they did not produce culturally
acceptable food products.
(E) producers were unwilling to alter their
production systems.

12. Which one of the following constitutes the
author's primary criticism of Anglo-American
economists' studies of technological
innovations?

(A) They do not understand that profit
motives have a major influence on
technology.
(B) They are biased in favor of technological
innovations.
(C) Their focus has been almost exclusively
on Western societies and cultures.
(D) They do not understand the role of Third
World governments in shaping economic
developments.
(E) They underestimate the importance of
sociocultural factors in analyzing
technological changes.

13. According to the passage, one can assume
that *triticale* is

(A) a nonliving form.
(B) an animal.
(C) a rock produced by grains of sand
subjected to pressure.
(D) a low form of animal life.
(E) a plant.

14. The tone of the author is

(A) hopelessness.   (D) reserved.
(B) pessimism.   (E) sarcastic.
(C) enthusiastic.

15. The author links progress in solutions of the food shortages most closely with

- (A) culture and technology.
- (B) economics and technology.
- (C) psychology and technology.
- (D) politics and culture.
- (E) government and technology.

16. In meeting food needs among the various segments of the populations within the developing countries, the author places highest regard on

- (A) the elite improving their own positions.
- (B) equalizing economic power in developing countries.
- (C) ensuring food availability.
- (D) technical advances in food preparation.
- (E) technical advances in food technology.

Line
(1)   I need scarcely adduce further evidence of the fact that Anglophobia is still a power in the land, if not the power it once was. But active and aggressive Anglophobia is, I think, a less important factor in
(5) the situation than the sheer indifference to England, with a latent bias toward hostility, which is so widespread in America. To the English observer, this indifference is far more disconcerting than hatred. The average Briton, one may say with
(10) confidence, is not indifferent toward America. He may be very ignorant about it, very much prejudiced against certain American habits and institutions, very thoughtless and tactless in expressing his prejudices; but the United States is
(15) not, to him, a foreign country like any other, on the same plane with France, Germany, or Russia. But that is precisely what England is to millions of Americans—a foreign country like any other. We see this even in many travelling Americans; much
(20) more is it to be noted in multitudes who stay at home. Many Americans seem curiously indifferent even to the comfort of being able to speak their own language in England; probably because they have less false shame than the average Englishman
(25) in adventuring among the pitfalls of a foreign tongue. They—this particular class of travellers, I mean—land in England without emotion, visit its shrines without sentiment, and pass on to France and Italy with no other feeling than one of relief in
(30) escaping from the London fog. These travellers, however, are but single spies sent forth by vast battalions who never cross the ocean.

(Archer, William, *America To-Day*. New York: Charles Scribner's Sons, 1899, pp. 174–175.)

17. The author likens American visitors to England to

- (A) American visitors to other countries.
- (B) travellers from other countries.
- (C) infiltrators.
- (D) those exploring their genealogy.
- (E) enthusiastic visitors from any other country.

18. The most important reaction of Americans to the English is

- (A) fear.
- (B) indifference.
- (C) activism.
- (D) aggressiveness.
- (E) open hostility.

19. The writer says that the English

- (A) suffer from Anglophobia.
- (B) are indifferent toward Mexicans.
- (C) are disconcerted toward Americans.
- (D) feel hatred toward Americans.
- (E) are indifferent toward Americans.

20. The writer indicates that the English are not

- (A) ignorant toward America.
- (B) prejudiced against American habits and institutions.
- (C) hesitant in expressing prejudices.
- (D) tactless in expressing prejudices.
- (E) likely to consider America just another foreign country.

21. Americans do not tend to

- (A) regard England as a foreign country.
- (B) stay at home—an indication that they regard England as a foreign country.
- (C) be indifferent to the "Mother Country" of many Americans.
- (D) have less false shame than the average Englishman about not speaking a foreign language.
- (E) visit shrines in England with emotion.

22. In the passage, the word *Anglophobia* means

- (A) love of angels.
- (B) love of England.
- (C) love of America.
- (D) fear of England.
- (E) fear of America.

Line
(1)   The liberty of a people consists in being
governed by laws which they have made
themselves, under whatsoever form it be of
government; the liberty of a private man in being
(5)   master of his own time and actions, as far as may
consist with the laws of God and of his country.
Of this latter only we are here to discourse, and
to inquire what estate of life does best suit us in
the possession of it. This liberty of our own
(10) actions is such a fundamental privilege of human
nature, that God Himself, notwithstanding all His
infinite power and right over us, permits us to
enjoy it, and that, too, after a forfeiture made by
the rebellion of Adam. He takes so much care for
(15) the entire preservation of it to us, that He suffers
neither His providence nor eternal decree to
break or infringe it. Now for our time, the same
God, to whom we are but tenants-at-will for the
whole, requires but the seventh part to be paid to
(20) Him at as a small quitrent, in acknowledgment of
His title. It is man only that has the impudence to
demand our whole time, though he neither gave
it, nor can restore it, nor is able to pay any
considerable value for the least part of it. This
(25) birthright of mankind above all other creatures
some are forced by hunger to sell, like Esau, for
bread and broth; but the greatest part of men
make such a bargain for the delivery up of
themselves, as Thamar did with Judah; instead of
(30) a kid, the necessary provisions for human life,
they are contented to do it for rings and
bracelets. The great dealers in this world may be
divided into the ambitious, the covetous, and the
voluptuous; and that all these men sell
(35) themselves to be slaves—though to the vulgar it
may seem a Stoical paradox—will appear to the
wise so plain and obvious that they will scarce
think it deserves the labour of argumentation.

      (Cowley, Abraham. *Essays*, London: Cassell
and Company, 1893, pp. 13–15.)

23. The author says that the freedom of an
individual

(A) is being master of his own time and actions.
(B) is limited by laws of God and country.
(C) necessarily consists of being governed by
laws made by himself.
(D) is being master of his own time and actions
but limited by laws of God and country.
(E) was forfeited by the rebellion of Adam.

24. The writer's feeling toward freedom is

(A) a very conservative viewpoint.
(B) enthusiastic and supporting at all costs.
(C) that eventually there will always be slaves
who sell themselves for such things as
ambition.
(D) one of warning.
(E) that it is a privilege.

25. The writer states that God

(A) demands forfeiture of freedom as a result of
Adam.
(B) requires a tithe of one-tenth of our freedom.
(C) requires one-seventh of our freedom.
(D) permits us to enjoy freedom but can take it
away.
(E) can infringe on freedom by providence or
eternal decree.

26. The writer seems to believe that

(A) government in whatsoever form it be limits
freedom.
(B) being governed by laws limits the liberty of a
people.
(C) other people in power should be able to
demand freedom from those beneath them.
(D) freedom is like a birthright.
(E) freedom is a birthright which should be
bought and sold.

27. In regard to power, the writer cautions that:

(A) it can cost one's birthright.
(B) it can be restored.
(C) it is the birthright of mankind.
(D) it can be costly to those in power.
(E) humans sell it for hunger.

28. The writer would probably compare a human's
relation to God as that

(A) of a landlord and a tenant.
(B) of an apple and a worm.
(C) of a sharecropper and a landowner.
(D) of a slave to an owner.
(E) of a king to a subject.

29. The intention of the article is to

(A) discuss government and laws.
(B) advocate a religious doctrine.
(C) show the importance of individual freedom.
(D) show that freedom is a responsibility.
(E) indicate that freedom today has been forfeited.

30. Freedom should be

(A) bought and sold.
(B) earned.
(C) a privilege.
(D) a bargaining tool.
(E) relinquished by those in power.

31. Others should not demand the relinquishment of freedom because they

(A) did not give it.
(B) are not in hunger.
(C) are not in power.
(D) have no rings or bracelets.
(E) are covetous.

32. In the passage, the word *voluptuous* means

(A) sexy.   (D) unfair.
(B) extravagant.   (E) unworthy.
(C) greedy.

Line
(1)   The Celtic blood, military education, and slave-holding experiences of Mr. [Jefferson] Davis will easily explain the chief points in his intellectual and moral constitution. He saw very clearly, but not
(5) deeply. He was logical rather than intuitive, and possessed little real imagination. From given premises he reasoned with great exactness, but had neither the inductive power nor the power of insight necessary to the discovery of the principles
(10) or axioms upon which he based his syllogisms. The letter of the Constitution, as the fathers made it and understood it, was his political bible, and he manifested nowhere the slightest appreciation of the consideration that the fathers might have failed
(15) to give exact expression, in the instrument, to the political and social conditions of the country, or of the consideration that those conditions might have so changed through the natural course of human development as to require either a revision of the
(20) instrument or the employment of methods of liberal interpretation, such as would enable the political forces and ideas, existing at any given moment, to find some expression through it. He

ridiculed the idea of the "higher law," which is only
(25) an unfortunate name for a profound truth, the truth that jurisprudence has its basis in ethics, and must develop with the unfolding of the common consciousness of right and wrong. Mr. Davis's rhetoric corresponded in character closely with his
(30) logic. It was pure, perspicuous, and rather terse. It must have been a great relief to the Senate, after listening to the ornate sentences, mixed metaphors, and far-fetched similes of most of the Southern members, to have Mr. Davis tell them briefly,
(35) plainly, and distinctly, just what it was all about.

(Burgess, John W., *The Civil War and the Constitution*. New York: Charles Scribner's Sons, 1906, pp. 16–17.)

33. The author says that Jefferson Davis

(A) can be easily explained.
(B) did not appreciate the constitution—even slightly.
(C) did not believe in God—a higher law.
(D) was illogical.
(E) lacked a political bible.

34. Jefferson Davis was

(A) in favor of emancipation.
(B) lacking in depth.
(C) intuitive.
(D) able to develop axioms for syllogisms.
(E) lacking in ethics.

35. The writer states that

(A) Davis upheld the Constitution.
(B) Davis recognized the changes that had occurred—especially in the South—since the passing of the Constitution.
(C) employed the methods of liberal interpretation.
(D) Davis's logic and rhetoric lacked correspondence.
(E) Davis used ornate sentences.

36. The writer seems to

(A) give some moderate support of Davis and his views.
(B) be an enthusiastic supporter of Davis.
(C) present an unfavorable image of Davis.
(D) present Davis as an illustrious leader.
(E) have no interest in or respect for Jefferson Davis.

37. In regard to reasoning, Davis used best
   (A) inductive thinking.
   (B) deductive thinking.
   (C) premises he developed.
   (D) generalizations he developed.
   (E) his power of insight.

38. The writer would probably compare Davis's rhetoric with

   (A) a telegram.
   (B) a monologue.
   (C) free-thought verse.
   (D) literature rich in similes and ornate sentences.
   (E) something unfathomable.

39. The intention of the article is to

   (A) present the views of the Confederacy.
   (B) explain, in part, the loss of the Civil War by the Confederates.
   (C) present a view of Davis before his becoming Confederate President.
   (D) present an objective view of Davis.
   (E) indicate Davis's shortcomings.

40. Other senators probably

   (A) did not understand Davis's perspicuous speeches.
   (B) disliked Davis's far-fetched similes.
   (C) never knew how Davis stood on an issue.
   (D) feared Davis's liberal interpretation of the laws and Constitution.
   (E) considered Davis a conservative.

Reading Comprehension Drill
ANSWER KEY

1. (B)	21. (E)
2. (D)	22. (D)
3. (A)	23. (D)
4. (E)	24. (E)
5. (B)	25. (C)
6. (E)	26. (D)
7. (A)	27. (D)
8. (B)	28. (C)
9. (B)	29. (C)
10. (C)	30. (C)
11. (D)	31. (A)
12. (E)	32. (B)
13. (E)	33. (A)
14. (D)	34. (B)
15. (A)	35. (A)
16. (B)	36. (C)
17. (C)	37. (B)
18. (B)	38. (A)
19. (C)	39. (D)
20. (E)	40. (E)

Attacking Analytical Reasoning Questions

The Analytical Reasoning section on the LSAT is a 35-minute segment with four separate problems and 22–24 questions, puzzles, or mind teasers based on the four problems. The purpose of the Analytical Reasoning Section is to provide a measure of your ability to determine the structure of relationships and to draw conclusions. This type of problem solving often requires deductive reasoning: proceeding from the general to the specific. Deductive reasoning simulates the analyses of relationships required for the successful solving of legal problems.

Important Information!

The format of Analytical Reasoning questions consists of three parts: a paragraph that gives the facts for the question; a series of statements or conditions based on the paragraph; and a series of questions which requires you to use the conditions to predict the outcome.

The Directions

You should study the directions ahead of time. This will prevent your having to take time to study them on the day of the test. On test day you should be able just to skim quickly the instructions during the exam to refresh your memory. Take a few moments now to study the directions for the Analytical Reasoning section of the LSAT.

> <u>DIRECTIONS:</u> Each group of questions in this section is based on a set of conditions. In answering some of the questions, it may be useful to draw a rough diagram. Choose the response that most accurately and completely answers each question and blacken the corresponding space on your answer sheet.

Analytical Reasoning Questions

Analytical Reasoning questions can better be understood by thinking of them as logic puzzles. There are two parts to a logic puzzle. First, conditions are described. Second, a task—such as scheduling a group meeting, arranging colored beads on a necklace, selecting players for a baseball team, or distributing information among several branches of a company—has to be performed. These tasks make up the questions of Analytical Reasoning logic puzzles.

In all Analytical Reasoning logic puzzles, conditions that restrict how the task can be performed (or how the questions are answered) are provided. Consider the following example:

Six colored beads—blue, red, white, green, yellow, and orange—are arranged on a necklace.

The blue bead has to follow the red bead.

The blue bead can only be either the second or fourth bead.

Bust it!

1. **Which of the following is a possible arrangement of the beads?**

   (A) Orange, white, red, yellow, green, blue

   (B) Blue, red, white, orange, green, yellow

   (C) White, red, green, blue, yellow, orange

   (D) Red, yellow, blue, white, orange, green

   (E) Red, white, green, yellow, blue, orange

The first part of this logic puzzle consists of the conditions or relationships among the objects involved in the question. In this example, the conditions establish a relationship between blue and red beads and the relationship of the blue bead to all the beads on the necklace. The conditions define the possible placement of the beads, limiting the number of ways in which the task can be performed.

The first condition defines fixed relationships: The blue bead always follows the red bead. The second condition defines a variable relationship: The blue bead can be placed either second or fourth among the beads.

Bust it!

Since the conditions established contain a variable relationship, the conditions don't completely define the outcome of the question. This is a common premise for Analytical Reasoning questions. The problem you are faced with in the questions determines the outcome as answer choices conform to the conditions.

There are usually three or four questions for each set of conditions. In our example, we will focus on just one question.

Our sample question requires you to determine a fixed relationship. The correct answer can easily be deduced from the conditions. To answer the question, simply look at the answer choices and eliminate the ones that don't follow the rules set in the conditions:

You can eliminate choices (A), (D), and (E) because they don't follow the second condition (the blue bead isn't in the second or fourth place). Choice (B) does not adhere to either condition and can also be eliminated. Therefore, choice (C) is your correct answer.

Bust it!

As we stated before, most Analytical Reasoning logic puzzles ask you to perform a task based on variable relationships. Our first example was based on a fixed relationship. Let's now look at a variable relationship question, based on the same conditions as our first example, since these are much more common the LSAT:

> Six colored beads—blue, red, white, green, yellow, and orange—are arranged on a necklace.
>
> The blue bead has to follow the red bead.
>
> The blue bead can only be either the second or fourth bead.
>
> 2.   If the white bead must be placed next to the blue bead, which of the following statements must be true?

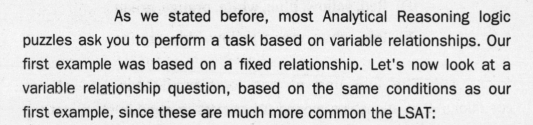

(A) The blue bead cannot be second.

(B) The white bead cannot be first.

(C) The white bead has to be between the red and blue beads.

(D) The white bead cannot be fifth.

(E) The red and blue beads cannot be next to each other.

One way to easily identify a variable-relationship question is the presence of the word *if* in the question. Often, variable-relationship questions provide additional information and then ask you to reach a conclusion about how a task can be performed using both the established conditions and the additional information provided in the question.

Bust it!

To answer this second example, you must combine the information in the conditions and the question. If you do this, you arrive at the following conditions to use in the question. You should only use these conditions for this question. **Subsequent or previous questions do not adhere to the additional information presented in the question you are working on.** Here are your combined conditions for this second example:

The red bead precedes the blue bead

The white bead is next to the blue bead

The blue bead is either in second or fourth place

Consider the implications of these conditions: If the blue bead is fourth, the white bead has to be either third or fifth. You also know that the red bead has to precede the blue bead, therefore, if blue is second, red has to be first, and white has to be third.

Look!

Important Strategy

Bust it!

Now look at the answer choices. Choice (A) states that the blue cannot be second and directly contradicts one of the conditions and can be eliminated. Choice (B) states that white cannot be first. As we have deduced before looking at the choices, this is true. So keep choice (B) for now. Choice (C) presents a statement that is not necessarily true based on the conditions. Since it is not necessarily true, choice (C) is probably not the correct answer, but don't throw it out just yet. Moving on to choices (D) and (E), you can see they present statements that also contradict the conditions and thus can be eliminated. As you can see below, the white bead can be fifth (D) and the red and blue bead can be next to each other (E):

R   B   W
____   ____   ____   ____   ____   ____

After looking at the answer choices, you've eliminated all but two of the choices. Choice (B) is always true. Choice (C) is not necessarily true. The white bead does not have to be between the red and blue beads:

Bust it!

R   G   Y   B   W   O
____   ____   ____   ____   ____   ____

Since we are looking for the best answer to the question, you should select choice (B) since it is always true—a much better answer than one that may or may not be true.

As you can see, no special skills such as formal logic or mathematics are necessary for solving the logic puzzles in the Analytical Reasoning section. You can answer the questions by focusing on the information provided by the conditions, deducing information that is implicit in the conditions, and carefully applying any new information that might be provided by the questions.

In the following sections, we will present a detailed approach to answer any type of Analytical Reasoning question and also strategies for studying conditions, organizing and visualizing the information, and how to approach the common logic puzzles presented in the Analytical Reasoning section.

Testbusting Tip #1:
A STEP-BY-STEP APPROACH FOR ANSWERING ANALYTICAL REASONING LOGIC PUZZLES

Step 1: Carefully read the conditions one at a time.

Step 2: Determine exactly what each condition states.

Step 3: Determine what, if anything, each condition implies.

Step 4: Rewrite or symbolize each condition to make it easy for you to reference and work with.

Step 5: Consider the conditions as a whole and the relationships they establish between objects in the puzzle.

Step 6: Spend the time to completely understand the conditions before moving on to the questions.

Step 7: Answer the questions, making sure to carefully apply any new information the questions present into the original conditions.

Important Strategy

STEP 1 | Read the conditions one at a time.

Important Strategy

All conditions are written in a straightforward way, even though sometimes they may appear convoluted. **The conditions are not**

meant to trick you. Therefore, don't worry about hidden meanings. Read the conditions to understand what they mean and what they imply.

> ## STEP 2 | Determine exactly what each condition states.

It is essential that you pay particular attention to words that describe or restrict relationships. Words such as *at least, immediately, exactly, only, always, never, must be, cannot be,* and so on, play a crucial role in the conditions you are to understand. Learn to pick out such words in the conditions and how they apply to the puzzle in general without making unwarranted assumptions. For instance, in our first example, the conditions stated that in a necklace of six colored beads, the blue bead has to follow the red bead. In reading a condition such as this, don't assume that the blue bead has to come directly after the red bead. The condition doesn't say that; it simply states that the blue bead can't come before the red bead.

> ## STEP 3 | Determine what, if anything, each condition implies.

You must find out if there is any useful information implicit (or unstated), in each condition. Often, additional information can be deduced from a given condition.

Let's continue looking at our first example. You know that there are six colored beads and that the blue bead must follow the red bead. Can you deduce anything from this condition? Yes, you can. Since the blue bead has to follow the red bead, the blue bead can't be the first bead on the necklace. Also, the red bead can't be last on the necklace. By deducing these two points, you've reduced the number of possible arrangements on the necklace. And you haven't even looked at the questions yet!

Be careful when looking for implicit information. Not all conditions will yield additional information through deduction. Many conditions are limited to explicit statements. So don't spend unnecessary time looking for information that isn't there.

STEP 4 | Rewrite or symbolize each condition to make it easy for you to reference and work with.

One of the major challenges in answering Analytical Reasoning questions is keeping track of all the conditions. Our example so far has been relatively simple in the number or complexity of its conditions. **It is very time-consuming to keep re-reading the conditions, yet it is essential to return to them as you consider each question. The best solution to this quandary is to rewrite the conditions in way that you can quickly glance at and remember.**

Important Strategy

Although there is no single system for rewriting the conditions, a good method is to symbolize each condition. **This is when your scrap paper that was given to you before you began the LSAT becomes invaluable. Scrap paper is essential to successfully attack the LSAT Analytical Reasoning section.** First, substitute initials for the names of objects or subjects in the conditions. Don't be concerned or confused. The LSAT writers almost always use objects or subjects that start with different letters of the alphabet.

Second, select symbols to represent relationships. Mathematical symbols such as "=," ">," and so on, can be useful. You can also devise your own symbols. Whatever method you use, make sure that the symbols are meaningful to you.

To use our sample question again, you could represent the condition that dictates that the blue bead must follow the red bead as:

R > B or R before B

You also need to symbolize the implicit information you deduced from the condition. Thus, you can write:

B ≠ 1 and R ≠ 6

or

B not 1 and R not 6

Either notation tells you at a glance that the blue bead can't be first and the red bead can't be last.

*Important
Strategy*

Keep your notations neat. Rewrite all the conditions in one area of your scrap paper. Arrange the conditions logically in a way that will make it easy for you to refer to them. Write clearly. Do all of your other work on a question away from the conditions so you will not get confused.

Drawing diagrams is an essential component to rewriting and symbolizing conditions. So important, that we gave creating diagrams its own section that follows later on. When drawing a diagram, you will apply your rewriting and symbolizing skills. So practicing rewriting and symbolizing will help you create better diagrams.

Step 5	Consider the conditions as a whole and the relationships they establish between objects in the puzzle.

Once you've studied the conditions individually and have rewritten and symbolized them, you should consider the conditions as a whole. **Often, when conditions are combined, additional information comes to light.**

Look!

Important Strategy

Look for conditions that deal with the same object or subject. These will be the conditions that will lend themselves to being combined. Put the conditions together and consider whether the combination provides any additional information.

Consider these conditions from our example:

The blue bead has to follow the red bead

The blue bead can only be either second or fourth

Both conditions state something about the blue bead. Therefore, we can try to combine them. If the blue bead can only be second or fourth, and if the red bead has to precede the blue bead, the red bead can only be either first, second, or third. You have now limited the number of possible arrangement of the beads even further.

Step 6	Spend the time to completely understand the conditions before moving on to the questions.

Look!

Important Strategy

Although the constraints that the LSAT places on the time you spend on each question make it seem that you should concentrate on the questions, this is not the case. Spend the majority of your time on the conditions. Understanding them thoroughly is the best way to answer more questions correctly and efficiently.

Step 7	Answer the questions, making sure to carefully apply any new information the questions present into the original conditions.

Look!

Important Strategy

Once you completely understand the conditions—alone and together—and have gleaned and symbolized any additional information to be found, you are ready to answer the questions. Remember, each question is likely to add more information to the original conditions. Before answering such a question, carefully apply this information to your conditions and understand how this new information affects the relationships between the objects or subjects of the puzzle. Only then should you attempt to answer the question.

 Testbusting Tip #2
DIAGRAMMING ANALYTICAL REASONING QUESTIONS

Even after you understand all the conditions, their implications, and the relationships among them, there is still a lot of information to deal with. What you need is a way to pull all of this information together to help you see the different ways in which the questions can be answered. Rewriting and symbolizing the conditions is a step in that direction. But using your scrap paper to diagram is the best way to achieve this ability to look at the overall picture for each Analytical Reasoning question.

Important Strategy

Diagrams provide a way to combine the information in the conditions so that you can clearly see what options and alternatives are available within the constraints of the conditions.

You should construct a diagram after, and only after, you have done all the work with the conditions that we've previously outlined. **To create a diagram before you completely understand the conditions and all their implications and relationships would be a waste of time. Your goal in creating diagrams should be to incorporate as much of the available information into one cohesive picture. If you create a diagram before you know all the information, that diagram will be incomplete and useless.**

Important Strategy

To diagram, you should start by visualizing the situation and deciding what kind of diagram would be most useful. For instance, in a logic puzzle that asks you to schedule a meeting between several people, a chart listing the participants and the times they can and can't meet is very helpful. If a logic puzzle asks you to arrange people around a table, it is useful to draw the shape of the table that is specified in the conditions. The conditions in logic puzzles are always very precise about defining the physical attributes of objects or subjects. Remember, the point of a diagram is to give yourself a visual frame of reference for the logic puzzle.

The second step of diagramming is to begin to incorporate the available information into the diagram. Start with concrete information. For instance, if you were to draw a diagram using the necklace of beads in our previous example, you could probably start

by drawing six dashes to represent the positions of the six beads on the necklace. Then, you would place the blue bead, since you have a condition that tells you the only two possible positions for the blue bead. Such a diagram would look like the following:

        B

_____ _____ _____ _____ _____ _____

or

                    B

_____ _____ _____ _____ _____ _____

Once you've created your diagram and have used all the concrete information, look at the conditions that provide information about relationships. In our example, such a condition is the one that states that the blue bead has to follow the red bead. You can use this information to refine your diagram. Now you have four possible arrangements:

   R   B

_____ _____ _____ _____ _____ _____

or

   R   B

_____ _____ _____ _____ _____ _____

or

         R   B

_____ _____ _____ _____ _____ _____

or

               R   B

_____ _____ _____ _____ _____ _____

As you can see, you would need further information from conditions or from questions to determine a possible arrangement of all the beads.

Because this example is simple, it didn't take long to diagram all of the options. **In constructing diagrams for more complex puzzles, don't spend time trying to create such a definitive diagram. The diagram is a framework that incorporates all the concrete information given in the conditions. Draw a new diagram for each question that gives new information. Leave the original intact so you can refer to it again and again to create new diagrams for each question. Remember to use information provided in a question for that question only. And always remain aware of the original conditions.**

Important Strategy

It is difficult to create diagrams for some puzzles. In such cases, try to represent at least part of the information in your diagram. **Don't spend too much time figuring out how to create the diagram. As we said before, concentrate on the understanding and figuring out the implications and relationships of the conditions.**

Testbusting Tip #3:
RECOGNIZING AND UNDERSTANDING
COMMON LOGIC PUZZLES

Although logic puzzles come in many different forms, the majority of them fall into three basic types based on the tasks that they require you to perform:

Important Strategy

1. **Sequence puzzles**

2. **Group puzzles**

3. **Map puzzles**

The best way to understand and prepare for these types of logic puzzles is look at examples of each and learn how to best approach them.

Sequence Puzzles

Sequence puzzles ask you to arrange things in sequential order (one after another). Our previous example of the beads on a necklace is a very elementary sequence puzzle. Arranging objects is a common task in sequence puzzles.

You can be asked to arrange lots of things, such as people, animals, numbers, or values. For example, a sequence puzzle might ask you to place five people, one to a floor, in a five-story building. Notice that in this case you would be creating a vertical sequence. Most people tend to think of sequences in a linear fashion, but don't let that confuse you. A vertical sequence is also linear, only the direction is different.

Still other sequence puzzles ask you to arrange events. The difference here is that you are arranging things in time. Whatever the actual task, the strategies for all sequence puzzles are the same.

The conditions of sequence games focus on the location of objects within the sequence and on the location of objects relative to each other. You saw this in the beaded necklace example, where you were told that the blue bead had to be second or fourth and that the red bead had to precede the blue bead.

Important Information!

When working with the conditions of sequence puzzles, begin with the conditions that give you the location of an object in the sequence. Then proceed to the conditions that specify relative location. Pay very close attention to words that define or restrict relative positions. In sequence puzzles in particular, words such as *preceding, following, immediately,* and *next to* are very important.

The following example will illustrate how a sequence game should be approached. Pay careful attention to how the conditions are analyzed, how they are symbolized, and how a diagram is created.

Seven soccer players are to be honored at a banquet. The players will be seated along one side of a rectangular table.

Allen and Barry have to leave the party early and so must be seated to the extreme right end of the table, which is closest to the exit.

Chuck will receive a plaque and so must be in the center chair to facilitate the presentation.

Dirk and Ed, who are bitter rivals for the position of goalkeeper during the season, dislike one another and should be seated as far apart as possible.

Frank and Gary are best friends and want to sit together.

Bust it!

1. Which of the following players may not be seated at either end of the table?

    (A) Dirk   (D) Gary

    (B) Ed   (E) Allen

    (C) Barry

2. Which of the following pairs of players may not be seated together?

    (A) Gary and Ed   (D) Barry and Ed

    (B) Chuck and Ed   (E) Frank and Dirk

    (C) Frank and Allen

3.   If neither Frank nor Ed is seated next to Chuck, how many different seating arrangements are possible?

     (A) 1   (D) 4

     (B) 2   (E) 5

     (C) 3

You should begin by examining the conditions to see if any of them give you concrete information about the locations of the soccer players. At first glance, Condition One only gives you the relative locations of Allen and Barry. If you look at the condition more closely, however, it does tell you fairly specifically where these two players will be seated. They will be next to each other in the two chairs at the right end of the table.

Bust it!

For the sake of convenience, you can number the seats. You have seats 1 through 7, from left to right. Now you can say that Allen and Barry will be in seats 6 and 7. You don't know, however, precisely which seat each player will occupy. You can rewrite this condition as follows:

$$A = 6 \text{ and } B = 7$$

or

$$A = 7 \text{ and } B = 6$$

Condition Two gives you even more concrete information than Condition One. Condition Two states precisely which seat Chuck will occupy. It can be rewritten as:

$$C = 4$$

Condition Three provides information about the relative locations of Dirk and Ed. This is a particularly ambiguous condition since it doesn't clearly specify where the two players have to be in relation to each other. All it says is that they have to be seated as far apart as possible. The only inferences you can make from this is that Dirk and Ed cannot be seated next to each other and that, given two options, you should select the option that places the players farthest apart.

Bust it!

Condition Three is difficult to symbolize. The best approach in a case like this is to write the important information in the condition on your scrap paper. In this example, you could write the names of the players and the part of the sentence that states that they should be seated as far apart as possible.

Condition Four tells you that Frank and Gary want to sit together. Do not assume that because the condition doesn't say that they *must* sit together, it is not a necessary condition. This is a trap laid by the LSAT writers. Condition Four says, in a deliberately ambiguous way, that the two players will sit together. You can rewrite this condition as:

FG or GF

You can infer an additional piece of information from Condition Four. Since Frank and Gary should sit together, neither one of them can be seated in seat 5, between Chuck and Allen or Barry. This can be written as:

F ≠ 5 and G ≠ 5

You can also combine Conditions Three and Four to get further information. Neither Frank nor Gary can be in seat 5. Therefore, either Dirk or Ed has to sit in seat 5. Furthermore, because Frank and

Gary have to sit together, the remaining positions for Dirk and Ed are seat 1 and seat 3. And since they have to be placed as far apart as possible, seat 1 is the preferred alternative. Therefore, you can write:

$$D = 5 \text{ or } E = 5$$

and

$$D = 1 \text{ or } E = 1$$

This, in turn, can be rewritten as

$$D = 1 \text{ and } E = 5$$

or

$$D = 5 \text{ and } E = 1$$

Now you can begin to build a diagram. Since the table or its shape is not important to the outcome of the puzzle, you don't need to include it in the diagram. Instead, you should use seven numbered dashes representing the seats.

_____   _____   _____   _____   _____   _____   _____
  1   2   3   4   5   6   7

Chuck should be placed first since you know his exact location,

                         C
_____   _____   _____   _____   _____   _____   _____
  1   2   3   4   5   6   7

Now you can place Allen and Barry,

or

1	2	3	4	5	6	7
			C		A	B

1	2	3	4	5	6	7
			C		B	A

You can see that it would be very time-consuming to diagram all of the alternatives. Instead, you can summarize the possibilities in a seat chart:

S1	S2	S3	S4	S5	S6	S7
D or E	F or G	F or G	C	D or E	A or B	B or E

You can now turn to the questions.

Question 1 asks which of the five listed players—Dirk, Ed, Barry, Gary, or Allen—cannot sit at either end of the table. In other words, which player cannot occupy either seat 1 or seat 7. All of the seating options are listed in the chart you have created. The chart clearly shows that of the five players listed in the question, only Gary cannot sit in seats 1 or 7. Therefore, the correct answer choice is (D).

Bust it!

Question 2 asks which two players cannot sit next to each other. The best approach to questions of this type—ones that ask which of the answer choices cannot be true—is to see how each choice could be true. In this question, choice (A) could be true if Ed were in seat 1 and Gary in seat 2. You can eliminate choice (A). Since Chuck has to be in seat 4, choice (B) could be true if Ed were in seat 5. Eliminate choice (B). Choice (C) is a bit more complex. For Allen to have anyone other than Barry next to him, he has to be in seat 6 (Barry is then in seat 7). For Frank and Allen to be next to each other, Frank would have to be in seat 5. Frank being seated in seat 5 would violate the condition that he and Gary have to sit together. Therefore, Frank

*Important
Strategy*

and Allen cannot sit together, and choice (C) is the correct choice. Once you are certain that you have the right answer, go on to the next question. Don't spend time second-guessing yourself.

Question 3 gives you the locations of Frank and Ed. You know that the possible places for Frank are seats 2 and 3. If Frank is not next to Chuck, who is in seat 4, Frank must be in seat 2. Ed, on the other hand, must be in seat 1 or 5. If he is not next to Chuck, Ed must be in seat 1. You now know the exact sequence of the first five players at the table: Ed, Frank, Gary, Chuck, and Dirk. Both Allen and Barry, however, can sit in either seat 6 or seat 7. Therefore, the information provided by Question 3 allows you to narrow down the possibilities to two arrangements. Thus, choice (B) is your correct answer.

From this example you can see that it pays to spend time understanding all aspects of the conditions. When you got to the questions, there was still a little work to do, but understanding the conditions put you in control and helped you think efficiently and quickly to get the correct answers.

Group Puzzles

As the name implies, the task in group puzzles is forming groups. For example, you might be asked to select players for a team or to distribute several books between two shelves. There are, in fact, two types of group games:

*Important
Information!*

1. Those that ask you to assemble one group

2. Those that ask you to divide the objects of the puzzle into several groups

There is no difference between how these two types of group puzzles should be approached. You should be aware of the distinction, however, and should be careful to stay aware of the type of task the particular group puzzle asks you to perform.

Another important feature of group puzzles is that in some of them, more objects or participants are presented in the conditions than are necessary to form the group. For instance, you might be asked to select four people for a committee out of seven available candidates. This feature is particular to group puzzles. All sequence and map puzzles (which you'll learn about next) use every available object or participant presented in the conditions.

Important Information!

It is essential when working with group puzzles that you remember whether you are using all of the objects or participants or only some of them. You should make this information part of your rewritten conditions. For instance, in the committee example we just mentioned, you would write:

Group = 4

at the beginning of your rewritten conditions. Forgetting how many participants can be included in the group is a major source of mistakes when tackling group puzzles.

The conditions of group puzzles focus on the interrelationships of the participants. Information is provided about which participants must be grouped together, which ones cannot be grouped together, and so on. This information is not always immediately accessible. **You should pay particular attention to implicit information and information derived by combining conditions.**

If/Then Conditions

Of special importance in group puzzles are "if/then" conditions. "If/then" conditions provide provisional information about

the participants of the puzzle. Let's look at an example where you are being asked to select five children for a school play. One of the conditions is:

If Peter is selected, then David cannot be selected.

Consider what this condition means. It is clear that if Peter is in the play, David is not. But does this condition mean anything else? What happens if David is in the play? If that is the case, Peter cannot be in the play. Otherwise the condition would be violated. You can actually write another condition based upon the one just stated:

If David is selected, then Peter cannot be selected.

So the reverse of our "if/then" condition is a condition in itself. This is true of all "if/then" conditions.

Now think about what happens if Peter is not selected. Does this mean that David must be selected? No, it doesn't. And David's not being in the play doesn't mean that Peter is in the play. The condition's requirement is that Peter and David are not in the play **together**. It says nothing about whether one or the other *must* be in the play. Be very careful in considering the implications of "if/then" conditions. Do not make unwarranted assumptions.

Another important aspect of "if/then" conditions is that they very often combine with other conditions to provide additional information. Look for participants mentioned in several conditions to see which of the conditions might be combined.

Let's do an example:

Mr. Warren is hiring five persons to do lawn care and tree pruning work on a landscaping project. He must

have a minimum of two people to care for the lawns. Nine persons have applied for the jobs: George, John, and Sam are lawn care workers, while Edgar, Alex, Rob, Walt, Bill, and Tom are tree pruners.

Mr. Warren is unwilling to hire Walt and Bill together because they argue all the time. Alex and Rob are buddies and will only work together. Sam won't work with Edgar because of their failure in a limited partnership effort.

1. If George, John, and Sam are hired, the team of tree pruners can consist of

   (A) only Alex and Rob.

   (B) Alex and Rob or Walt and Bill.

   (C) Walt and Tom or Bill and Tom.

   (D) Alex and Rob, or Walt and Tom, or Bill and Tom.

   (E) only Tom.

2. Mr. Warren has the greatest number of choices for hiring tree pruners if the lawn care workers he chooses are

   (A) George, John, and Sam.

   (B) Sam only.

   (C) George and John.

   (D) George and Sam.

   (E) John and Sam.

Bust it!

3. If Edgar is hired, the other persons hired must be

   (A) George, John, Alex, and Sam.

   (B) George, John, Sam, and either Walt, Bill, or Tom.

(C) George, John, Bill, and Walt.

(D) George and John, together with either Alex and Rob or Walt and Tom.

(E) George and John, together with either Alex and Rob, Walt and Tom, or Bill and Tom.

The first point you should notice is that you will be selecting five out of nine people. You should write this down on your scrap paper:

Group = 5

Second, you should notice that you have two types of participants: lawn care workers and tree pruners. When a group puzzle involves more than one type of participant, it's a good idea to devise a method to visually represent this. For instance, you can use lowercase initials for the lawn carers and capitals for the tree pruners. Thus, you have:

g, j, s and E, A, R, W, B, T

Finally, you must be aware of the fact that the group must have a minimum of two lawn care workers. Be careful not to misinterpret conditions such as this. A minimum of two lawn care workers doesn't mean *only* two. It means that you must have at least two lawn care workers, but that you could also have more (in this case you could have three). You can rewrite this condition in the following mathematical notation:

lawn care workers ≥ 2

Now you can move on to the conditions. Condition One is essentially an "if/then" condition that comes straight to the point: Walt and Bill cannot work together. This can be rewritten as

not W + B

Condition Two says that Alex and Rob must work together:

A + R

And Condition Three tells you that Sam and Edgar cannot work together:

not s + E

No two conditions deal with the same participants. Therefore, it is impossible to consider the conditions jointly (combine them). The information provided directly by the conditions is all you have to work with.

Since this is a relatively simple puzzle with few potential outcomes, the best way to build your diagram is to make a chart of possible groups. For more complex group puzzles, it's a good idea to write down the initials of the participants for each question and then cross out the ones that cannot be included.

Bust it!

Based on the conditions presented, there are four possible groups of lawn care workers in this example:

gjs   gj   gs   js

For each of these groups, several groups of tree pruners are possible. If George, John, and Sam are hired, only two tree pruners can be hired. Edgar cannot be hired because he and Sam cannot work together. Since Walt and Bill cannot work together, Alex and Rob have to work together. Thus the only possibilities if George, John, and Sam are hired are:

AR   WT   BT

If George and John are hired, three tree pruners have to be hired. Since Sam is not included, Edgar can be hired. You can find the possible combinations that include Edgar by simply adding him to the combinations you created above (when George, John, and Sam are hired). In essence you are exchanging Sam for Edgar. By doing so you have the following possibilities:

EAR   **EWT   EBT**

You can also make three combinations that do not include Edgar:

ARW   **ARB   ART**

Finally, if Sam is hired with either George or John, Edgar will not be hired, and you will have the same three-person teams of tree pruners as if George, John, and Sam are hired.

So, your complete list of combinations should look like this:

gjs	AR, WT, BT
gj	EAR, EWT, EBT, ARW, ARB, ART
gs	ARW, ARB, ART
gj	ARW, ARB, ART

Having completely read and understood the conditions, you can now turn to the questions.

Question 1 asks for the possible composition of the team of tree pruners if all three of the lawn care workers are hired. Having done all the hard work already, you can simply look at your comprehensive chart and determine that the correct answer is given in choice (D), Alex and Rob, or Walt and Tom, or Bill and Tom.

Question 2 asks which team of lawn care workers will give Mr. Warren the most flexibility in hiring the tree pruners. Consulting the chart again, you see that the correct choice is (C), George and John. Hiring Sam (A, B, D, and E) would limit Mr. Warren's choices of tree pruners since Sam won't work with Edgar. Also, if Mr. Warren hired three lawn care workers, he could only hire two, not three, tree pruners.

Finally, Question 3 asks who else must be hired if Edgar is hired. You can eliminate choices (A) and (B) since both answers include Sam and Edgar and it is stated that they cannot work together. You know from your chart that George and John must be hired in this case, along with either Alex or Rob, Walt or Tom, or Bill and Tom. Thus, the correct answer choice is (E).

Bust it!

Map Puzzles

The name "map puzzles" might be a little misleading. You probably think of maps as tools that tell you where streets, towns, cities, and countries are located. In map puzzles, although you will be using "maps," you will not be interested in the locations of places or things, but rather in how these places or things are connected. **What you will actually be dealing with are "road maps," because map puzzles are designed to test your ability to understand and to keep track of relationships among members of a given set.**

Important Information!

Consider this example: There are seven terminals in an airport. The terminals are connected to each other by a system of moving sidewalks. You are given conditions that define the connections between the various terminals. There is two-way traffic between some terminals and one-way traffic between others. You are then asked to determine how you can get from one particular terminal to another, how many different routes there are between certain terminals, and so on.

Not all map puzzles are geographical in nature, like this example. Some of these puzzles involve the flow of information between people or organizations. The important thing to remember is that it is the relationships between the participants that are important.

The conditions of map puzzles fully describe the situation. In this respect, map puzzles are quite different from sequence and group puzzles. **Once all the conditions are analyzed, no ambiguity remains in a map puzzle.**

Important Information!

Diagrams are critical in map puzzles. In fact, the whole analysis of conditions boils down to building a diagram. In doing so, you should start with the person or object that is mentioned most often in the conditions. Then add the others into your diagram one at a time, paying particularly close attention to the connections between them. Watch for the directions in which things can travel between the participants or objects. Is the connection two-way or one-way? If it is one-way, in which direction is it? Use arrows in your diagram to keep track of this information.

Finally, keep your diagram neat. Try to organize it in such a way that you don't have confusing connections and a lot of convoluted arrows. If you build a diagram that is confusing, revise it so it is easier to work with. **Remember, time invested in understanding the conditions pays off when you answer the questions.**

Important Information!

Let's look at an example:

Five chemists participate in an international scientific conference in Boston, Massachusetts.

Asprey speaks Polish and French

Carter speaks Polish and English

Peters speaks English and French

Thomas speaks Russian and Polish

Shore speaks French and Russian

1.   Which of the following can act as an interpreter when Peters and Thomas wish to confer?

(A) Asprey

(B) Carter

(C) Shore

(D) Asprey and Carter

(E) Any of the other three chemists

2.   Which of the following cannot converse without an interpreter?

(A) Carter and Shore

(B) Asprey and Carter

(C) Asprey and Peters

(D) Carter and Thomas

(E) Asprey and Shore

Bust it!

3.   Of the languages spoken, the two that are least common are

(A) English and Polish

(B) English and Russian

(C) French and Polish

(D) French and English

(E) Russian and Polish

Before you begin building your diagram, you have to decide on notation. You could use capitals for the initials of the chemists and lowercase letters for the languages they speak. The languages are the connections in this map puzzle.

Bust it!

But where do you start? Each chemist is mentioned only once in the conditions, so you cannot start with the one who is mentioned the most often. In this example, you have to consider which of the participants will have the most connections to other participants. To determine this, you need to look at which language is spoken by the greatest number of chemists. Polish and French are each spoken by three chemists. English and Russian are each spoken by two chemists. Asprey speaks both Polish and French, and, therefore, Asprey will have connections to the greatest number of other chemists.

You should place Asprey at the center of your diagram and connect her to the two other chemists who speak Polish (the choice between Polish and French is completely arbitrary at this point since they are equal in terms of speakers).

Bust it!

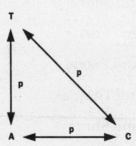

You can now place the other two people and complete the diagram by filling in all the connections:

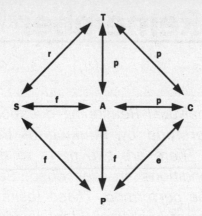

Now consider the questions. Question 1 asks which chemists can act as interpreters for Peters and Thomas. In other words, what is the connection between these people? It is clear from your map that Peters and Thomas are connected; they can speak to each other with the help of all the other chemists. Therefore, the correct answer is (E), any of the other three chemists.

Bust it!

Question Two asks which of the given pairs of chemists cannot speak without an interpreter. In terms of the diagram, you are looking for the two people who do not have a direct link. You know that Asprey is connected to everyone else. Therefore, you can eliminate choices (B), (C), and (E). Furthermore, you know that Carter is directly linked to Thomas but not to Shore. So choice (A) is the correct answer.

Finally, Question 3 asks which languages are least commonly used. You inadvertently answered this question when you were setting up the diagram. Polish and French are spoken by three people each, while Russian and English are spoken by only two people each. Thus, the correct answer choice is (B), Russian and English.

Bust it!

Points to Remember

✔ Analytical Reasoning questions can better be understood by thinking of them as logic puzzles. There are two parts to a logic puzzle. First, conditions are described. Second, a task has to be performed. These tasks make up the questions of Analytical Reasoning logic puzzles.

✔ In all Analytical Reasoning logic puzzles, conditions that restrict how the task can be performed (or how the questions are answered) are provided.

✔ In an argument, an assumption is a premise that isn't explicitly (directly) stated. These unstated premises are very important since the validity of an argument is determined by the validity of its assumptions. In other words, weaken an assumption and you can weaken the argument (and vice-versa).

✔ One way to easily identify a variable-relationship question is the presence of the word "if" in the question.

✔ Subsequent or previous questions do not adhere to the additional information presented in the question you are working on.

✔ No special skills such as formal logic or mathematics are necessary for solving the logic puzzles in Analytical Reasoning section. You can answer the questions by focusing on the information provided by the conditions, deducing information that is implicit in the conditions, and carefully applying any new information that might be provided by the questions.

On Target!

✔   *Understand and use the step-by-step approach for answering analytical reasoning logic puzzles.*

✔   *Scrap paper is essential to successfully attack the LSAT Analytical Ability Test because it enables you to symbolize, make notation, and create diagrams.*

✔   *Spend the majority of your time on the conditions. Understanding them thoroughly is the best way to answer more questions correctly and efficiently.*

✔   *Diagrams provide a way to combine the information in the conditions so that you can clearly see what options and alternatives are available within the constraints of the conditions.*

On Target!

✔   *Although logic puzzles come in many different forms, the majority of them fall into three basic types based on the tasks that they require you to perform: Sequence puzzles, Group puzzles, and Map puzzles.*

✔   *Sequence puzzles ask you to arrange things in sequential order (one after another).*

✔   *The task in group puzzles is forming groups. For example, you might be asked to select players for a team or to distribute several books between two shelves.*

✔   *Map puzzles are designed to test your ability to understand and to keep track of relationships among members of a given set.*

Drill: Analytical Reasoning

Questions 1–6 refer to the following.

The old-fashioned school buses had seats along each side. George, Ken, Ted, Arthur, Tory, and Lee are aboard the bus. The seats on the left side are numbered 1–3 and the seats on the right side are numbered 4–6.

Ted's seat is numbered two less than George's seat.

Ken is in seat 2 or seat 6.

If Ken is in 6, George is in 3, and Ted is in 5.

If Ken is in 2, Arthur is in 5.

1. If Tory's seat number is higher than Arthur's, what is true?

(A) Ted is in 6.   (D) Ted is in 3.
(B) Ted is in 1.   (E) Lee is in 4.
(C) Tory is in 5.

2. What must be true?

(A) Arthur's seat is lower than Ted's.
(B) Ted's seat is lower than Arthur's.
(C) Tory's seat is higher than Arthur's.
(D) Ken's seat number is lower than Lee's.
(E) Lee's seat number is higher than George's.

3. Who could sit in seat 2?

I.   Arthur
II. Ken
III. Ted
IV. Lee

(A) I and II only.   (D) III and IV only.
(B) II and IV only.   (E) I, II, and IV only.
(C) I and III only.

4. Tory cannot sit in which seat?

(A) Seat 1   (D) Seat 4
(B) Seat 2   (E) Seat 5
(C) Seat 3

5. If Tory is in seat 3, who is in seat 1?

(A) Lee   (D) Ken
(B) Ted   (E) George
(C) Arthur

6. If Ken is in seat 2, how many possible arrangements are there for the other passengers?

(A) 4   (D) 7
(B) 5   (E) 8
(C) 6

Questions 7–12 refer to the following.

The Chili China company makes thimbles. The clerk has been asked to display them in a seven-shelf cabinet. Two shelves will hold purple; two shelves will hold peach; one shelf will hold black; one shelf will hold blue; and one shelf will hold red. An acceptable display must meet these guidelines:

The first shelf must be peach.

The black shelf must not be directly above or below a peach shelf.

The red shelf must not be directly above or below a peach shelf.

The black shelf must be directly above the red shelf.

7. If, in an acceptable plan, the purple shelf is the second and fourth, which one of the following is determined?

(A) The third shelf will be blue.
(B) The fifth shelf will be black.
(C) The sixth shelf will not be blue.
(D) The seventh shelf will be peach.
(E) The sixth shelf will be black.

8. If, in an acceptable plan, a purple scheme is on the third and seventh shelves, which one of the following must be false?

    (A) Either the second shelf or the sixth shelf is blue.
    (B) Two peach shelves occur together.
    (C) The fifth shelf is black.
    (D) The blue shelf is above the black shelf.
    (E) The fourth shelf is peach.

9. Which one of these arrangements, from shelf 1 to 7, is acceptable?

    (A) Peach, blue, peach, purple, red, black, purple
    (B) Peach, blue, purple, peach, black, red, purple
    (C) Peach, purple, blue, purple, peach, red, black
    (D) Peach, blue, peach, purple, purple, red, black
    (E) Peach, purple, blue, black, red, peach, purple

10. If the red shelf is on shelf four, which one of the following could not be true?

    (A) Shelf two is black.
    (B) Shelf seven is purple.
    (C) Shelf six is purple.
    (D) Shelf five is blue.
    (E) Shelf five is black.

11. If the fourth shelf is black, which one of the following must be true?

    (A) Shelf five also holds black.
    (B) Shelf one holds purple.
    (C) Shelf five holds blue.
    (D) Shelf two holds black.
    (E) Shelf three holds red.

12. Which one of the following could be true?

    (A) Black is on shelf two.
    (B) Red is on shelf two.
    (C) Black is on shelf two and red is on shelf three.
    (D) Peach is on shelf two.
    (E) Red is on shelf three.

Questions 13–18 refer to the following.

A cook is preparing six dishes for six families. The families are the Martins, the Smiths, the Browns, the Rights, the Odums, and the Wrights. The six dishes are turkey, chicken pie, pork, ham, lamb, and salmon. There are just enough ingredients to prepare just one dish of each type.

The Smiths and the Odums do not eat pork.

The Rights always want salmon.

The Wrights will only eat lamb or pork.

The Martins will not eat pork or ham.

13. Which one of the following could be true?

    (A) The Martins get pork.
    (B) The Smiths get pork.
    (C) The Wrights get chicken pie.
    (D) The Odums get pork.
    (E) The Martins get lamb.

14. Which one of the following could be true?
    (A) The Rights get pork.
    (B) The Martins get ham.
    (C) The Wrights get ham.
    (D) The Wrights get salmon.
    (E) The Martins get pork.

15. If the Browns take the lamb and the Smiths take the turkey, what could the Odums take?

    I. Ham
    II. Chicken pie
    III. Salmon

    (A) I only.   (D) I or II only.
    (B) II only.   (E) I, II, and III.
    (C) III only.

16. If the Odums take the chicken pie, who will get the ham?

    (A) Smiths
    (B) Smiths or Browns
    (C) Browns only
    (D) Smiths or Martins
    (E) Wrights or Martins

17. If the Browns get the pork, what must be true?

(A) The Odums get the ham.
(B) The Smiths get the turkey or the chicken pie.
(C) The Smiths get the ham.
(D) The Martins get the pork.
(E) The Wrights get the lamb.

18. If the Martins get the lamb and the Browns get the chicken pie, what must be false?

(A) The Wrights get the pork.
(B) The Smiths get the pork.
(C) The Smiths get the turkey.
(D) The Odums get the turkey.
(E) The Odums get the ham.

Questions 19–25 refer to the following

The third-grade class is at Fun World. The rides include the Mickey Mouse Theatre, the Tree House, the Slippery Slide, the Banana Slide, the Jungle Cruise, the Snow White Theatre, and the Goofy Review.

Time is limited. The following rules have been set by the chaperones:

You may go on the Slippery Slide or the Banana Slide, but not both.

You may not go in the Mickey Mouse Theatre and on the Slippery Slide.

If you go in the Mickey Mouse Theatre, you must see the Goofy Review; if you go in the Goofy Review, you must see the Mickey Mouse Theatre.

If you go on the Tree House, you should go on the Banana Slide.

If you go on the Jungle Cruise, you should go on the Tree House or the Banana Slide, but not both.

19. If one child selects the Mickey Mouse Theatre, which one of the following must be true?

(A) The child will not select the Slippery Slide.
(B) The child will not select the Tree House.
(C) The child will select the Banana Slide.
(D) The child will select the Snow White Theatre.
(E) The child will not select the Jungle Cruise.

20. If a child chooses the Slippery Slide, what else may not be chosen?

(A) The Mickey Mouse Theatre
(B) The Tree House
(C) The Goofy Review
(D) The Jungle Cruise
(E) The Snow White Theatre

21. Which combination is inappropriate?

(A) Mickey Mouse and Goofy
(B) Tree House and Banana Slide
(C) Jungle Cruise and Banana Slide
(D) Mickey and Slippery Slide
(E) Jungle Cruise and Tree House

22. Which combination is appropriate?

(A) Tree House, but not Banana Slide
(B) Slippery Slide and Mickey Mouse Theatre
(C) Mickey Mouse Theatre, but not Goofy Review
(D) Jungle Cruise, Tree House, and Banana Slide
(E) Goofy Review and Mickey Mouse Theatre

23. Jane went in the Mickey Mouse Theatre. To follow the rules,

(A) she should go to the Slippery Slide.
(B) she should go to the Goofy Review.
(C) she could go to the Slippery Slide and the Goofy Review.
(D) she could go to the Tree House, but not the Banana Slide.
(E) she should go to the Banana Slide and the Slippery Slide.

24. If a child chooses the Tree House,

(A) the child could go on the Banana Slide and the Slippery Slide.
(B) the child could go on the Banana Slide, the Jungle Cruise, and the Tree House.
(C) the child could go on the Banana Slide and the Goofy Review alone.
(D) the child could go on the Banana Slide.
(E) the child could go in the Mickey Mouse Theatre and on the Banana Slide alone.

25. If a child chooses the Jungle Cruise, which one of the following can he/she also select?

I.   The Tree House.
II. The Banana Slide
III. The Mickey Mouse Theatre
IV. The Slippery Slide

(A) II and III only.   (D) I, II, and III only.
(B) III and IV only.   (E) I only.
(C) I and II only.

Questions 26–30 refer to the following

There are six children in the Davis family. None are the same age and all attend Mooresboro School. Mooresboro School offers classes for children from age four to 18. Children under 12 go to the main school. Children over 12 go to the portables.

Jerry is seven years younger than Pitt.

Norma is two years older than Jerry.

Carolyn is four years younger than Jerry.

Chris is one year younger than Tommy.

26. If Carolyn is five, how old is Pitt?

(A) 17   (D) 14
(B) 16   (E) 13
(C) 15

27. If Tommy is two years older than Norma, and Chris is 14, how old is Carolyn?

(A) Eleven   (D) Eight
(B) Ten   (E) Seven
(C) Nine

28. Which one of the following is a complete and accurate list of the children who could attend classes in the Mooresboro School portables?

(A) Norma, Chris, and Pitt
(B) Norma, Jerry, and Pitt
(C) Pitt, Chris, and Tommy
(D) Pitt, Norma, Tommy, and Chris
(E) Pitt and Norma

29. Who must attend classes in the Mooresboro School portables?

I.   Pitt
II. Norma
III. Chris
IV. Tommy

(A) I only.
(B) I and II only.
(C) I, II, and III only.
(D) All of the above.
(E) None of the above.

30. If Norma attends classes in the Mooresboro School portables what must be true?

(A) Jerry also attends classes in the portables
(B) Chris cannot be older than 16 years old.
(C) Chris is at least five years old.
(D) Carolyn is at least seven years old.
(E) Carolyn cannot be older than six years old.

Questions 31–36 refer to the following.

Albert, Bob, Charlie, Dirk, Edgar, and Frank are going to a playoff game in a distant city and have rented an eight-passenger van for the trip. One of the men always wears a red hat, another is nearsighted, one dislikes Frank, one wears a toupee, and one is Charlie's son.

The man who is wearing the toupee is the driver, and he is sitting next to Frank, who is sitting directly in front of Charlie's son.

Edgar is sitting next to the man who always wears a red hat.

Albert is sitting in the center seat of the second row.

The man who dislikes Frank is the only person sitting in the last row of the seats in the van.

The man who is nearsighted is seated directly behind Dirk, and Edgar is seated to Albert's right.

31. The person who always wears a red hat is

(A) Albert.   (D) Dirk.
(B) Bob.   (E) Edgar.
(C) Charlie.

32. The person who is Charlie's son is

(A) Albert.   (D) Dirk.
(B) Bob.   (E) Edgar.
(C) Frank.

33. The person who wears the toupee is

(A) Albert.   (D) Dirk.
(B) Bob.   (E) Edgar.
(C) Charlie.

34. The person who dislikes Frank could possibly be

(A) Albert.   (D) Dirk.
(B) Bob.   (E) Edgar.
(C) Frank.

35. The person who is sitting in the second row to the left could be

(A) Albert.   (D) Dirk.
(B) Bob.   (E) Edgar.
(C) Frank.

36. The person who could be sitting next to Frank is

(A) Albert.   (D) Dirk.
(B) Bob.   (E) Edgar.
(C) Frank.

Questions 37–40 refer to the following.

A television executive in charge of programming is considering two possible lineups of five new shows for the new season. When the lineups are completed, he will present both to the Vice President of Programming for approval. However, at present, only one lineup is completed; the other is only partially completed. The five new shows that will go into the lineups are the following: a news show, a situation comedy, a detective drama, a musical/variety show, and a nighttime soap.

Each show is an hour long, and the time slots are 6:00, 7:00, 8:00, 9:00, and 10:00.

In both of the lineups, the drama will be shown in the 7:00 time slot.

The news show will be on at 10:00 in only one of the lineups.

In both of the lineups, the nighttime soap will immediately follow the musical/variety show.

37. Which one of the following statements about the completed lineup is false?

(A) The situation comedy will be in the 6:00 time block.
(B) The musical/variety show will be in the 8:00 time block.
(C) The nighttime soap will be in the 9:00 time block.
(D) The situation comedy will be in the 8:00 time block.
(E) The news show will be in the 10:00 time block.

38. Which one of the following statements about the incomplete lineup is false?

(A) Either the news show or the situation comedy can appear in the 6:00 time block.
(B) Either the musical/variety show, the news show, or the situation comedy can appear in the 8:00 time block.
(C) Neither the situation comedy nor the news show can appear in the 9:00 time block.
(D) Either the situation comedy or the news show can appear in the 9:00 time block.
(E) The nighttime soap cannot appear in the 8:00 time block.

39. Which one of the following statements about the incomplete lineup is true?

(A) The detective drama comes on at 7:00.
(B) The soap comes on at 8:00.
(C) The soap comes on at 6:00.
(D) The musical/variety show comes on at 6:00.
(E) The musical/variety show comes on at 10:00.

40. Which one of the following statements about the completed lineup is true?

(A) The news show comes on at 7:00.
(B) The musical/variety show comes on at 6:00.
(C) The soap comes on at 7:00.
(D) The soap comes on at 8:00.
(E) The detective drama comes on at 7:00.

Analytical Reasoning Drill
ANSWER KEY

1. (B)	21. (D)
2. (B)	22. (E)
3. (E)	23. (B)
4. (B)	24. (D)
5. (A)	25. (E)
6. (A)	26. (B)
7. (C)	27. (E)
8. (E)	28. (D)
9. (D)	29. (A)
10. (A)	30. (B)
11. (E)	31. (A)
12. (D)	32. (E)
13. (C)	33. (D)
14. (D)	34. (B)
15. (D)	35. (B)
16. (B)	36. (D)
17. (E)	37. (A)
18. (B)	38. (E)
19. (A)	39. (A)
20. (A)	40. (E)

Chapter

Attacking
Logical
Reasoning
Questions

The Logical Reasoning questions on the LSAT measure your ability to understand and evaluate arguments. There are TWO Logical Reasoning sections on the LSAT. You will be given 35 minutes to complete each section and each section will have approximately 24-26 questions.

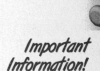

*Important
Information!*

Each Logical Reasoning question is based on arguments presented in short paragraphs. In most cases, each argument is followed by one question. Sometimes, two or more questions are based on one argument. The arguments are taken from a variety of fields, including the humanities, and social and physical sciences, as well as from sources such as advertisements and informal dialogues. **No specialized knowledge of formal logic or any subject is required to answer the questions.**

The Logical Reasoning questions focus on specific skills such as analyzing arguments, recognizing assumptions, drawing inferences, strengthening or weakening arguments, and evaluating the logic of arguments. The questions are designed to test your ability to understand the point the author tries to prove, to see what evidence the author uses to support the conclusion, to trace how the author gets from the evidence to the conclusion, and to judge the effectiveness of the argument.

*Important
Information!*

Since Logical Reasoning questions are designed to measure your ability to think logically and to evaluate the reasoning of others, the structure of an author's argument and the soundness of the method he or she uses are of primary importance. The actual idea or opinion the author expresses is essentially irrelevant. Do not base your answers on whether the author's point is true or false. A strong argument can be made to support a false conclusion; conversely, a weak argument may support a conclusion that is true. Concentrate on how the argument is made, not on its content.

In the following sections, we will discuss in detail the structure of an argument and common methods of argument. We will also explain how to evaluate arguments. And finally, we will discuss the types of questions you will encounter and the skills you need to practice for these questions. But first, let's look at the directions:

The Directions

You should study the directions ahead of time. This will prevent your having to take time to study them on the day of the test. On test day you should be able just to skim quickly the instructions during the exam to refresh your memory. Take a few moments now to study the directions for the Logical Reasoning questions on the LSAT.

> **DIRECTIONS:** The questions in this section are based on the reasoning contained in brief statements or passages. For some questions, more than one of the choices could conceivably answer the question. However, you are to choose the **best** answer; that is, the response that most accurately and completely answers the question. You should not make assumptions that are by common-sense standards implausible, superfluous, or incompatible with the passage. After you have chosen the best answer, blacken the corresponding space on your answer sheet.

Logical Reasoning Questions

The Argument

An argument is a line of reasoning designed to prove a point. Arguments can be simple, expressed in a few lines, or very complex, taking up whole books. Regardless of length and complexity, all arguments have the same basic framework: The author states some central idea, and then presents supporting evidence, laying it out in a logical pattern.

The central point of an argument is called the conclusion. Each piece of evidence used by the author is called a premise. And the way in which the premises are combined is called reasoning.

Important Information!

Premise:	All birds fly.
Premise:	Penguins are birds.
Conclusion:	Penguins fly.

The example presents a simple argument. The conclusion is based on two premises. If the premises are true, the conclusion must be true and the argument is valid. It is an unsound argument, however, since the first premise is false, all birds don't fly (like ostriches).

Note that a premise doesn't have to contain objective, factual evidence to support the conclusion. In fact, a premise doesn't even have to be true. A premise is any statement that the author uses to support the conclusion.

The first skill you need to practice for Logical Reasoning questions is identifying the conclusions and premises of arguments. The majority of arguments you will see are of two basic patterns:

(1) the conclusion follows the premises,

(2) the premises follow the conclusion.

The ability to quickly locate the conclusion and the premises is very important for doing well on Logical Reasoning questions.

Important Strategy

To identify the conclusion of an argument, ask yourself what central point the author is trying to make. What is the author trying to prove? Think about the one idea the author would want you to take away after reading the argument. That idea is the conclusion of the argument.

Certain structural words can help you locate the conclusion. Look for words such as:

therefore	thus
hence	consequently
accordingly	so
as a result	it follows
suggests	indicates

The premises of an argument are statements made by the author to support the conclusion. A statement, as we have said above, doesn't have to be factually true to be a premise.

Structural words that indicate a premise include the following:

Look!

Important Strategy

since	because
for	inasmuch as
insofar as	due to

Consider the following example and identify the conclusion and the premises.

Dogs make better pets than do cats. Dogs provide companionship and protection, whereas cats are more aloof and do not guard against intruders.

What is the central point of the argument? The author wants to prove that dogs are better pets than cats. Do not be fooled by conclusions that are phrased as statements of fact, as is the case in this example.

We can rewrite the argument as follows:

Premise: Dogs are better companions than cats.

Premise: Dogs guard against intruders, and cats do not.

Conclusion: Dogs make better pets than do cats.

With the argument in this form, it becomes clear how the author proceeds from the premises to the conclusion. Note that the actual sequence isn't important: The logic of the argument is the same whether the conclusion follows the premises or precedes them.

Important Strategy

There are some Logical Reasoning questions that directly ask you to identify the conclusion of an argument. These questions are usually worded in one of the following ways:

— Which of the following best summarizes the argument?

— The author's main point is...

To answer such a question, locate the conclusion of the argument in the way we discussed above and then select the answer choice which restates that conclusion.

Identifying the conclusion and the premises of an argument is the most important step in analyzing the argument. Therefore, the ability to locate the conclusions and premises of arguments is essential to answering almost all Logical Reasoning questions.

Recognizing and Using Assumptions

In an argument, an assumption is a premise that isn't explicitly (directly) stated. **These unstated premises are very important since the validity of an argument is determined by the validity of its assumptions. In other words, weaken an assumption and you can weaken the argument and vice-versa.**

Many Logical Reasoning questions deal with assumptions, either directly or indirectly. Therefore, it is extremely important that you practice recognizing assumptions in arguments.

Important Strategy

Assumptions are the missing links of arguments. You can think about assumptions in visual terms: Imagine the premises of an argument as spans of a bridge leading to the conclusion. An assumption—an unstated premise—is a missing span. The author takes for granted that it is there, but we can't see it. In considering an argument to find the underlying assumption, look for such missing links.

Let's look at an example. Try and identify the assumption the author has used in his or her argument.

Senator Franklin is a member of the Orange Party, which supports increased military spending by the Federal government. Franklin will surely vote for a cut in spending on social programs.

The argument assumes which of the following?

(A) Elected officials always support policies endorsed by their parties.

(B) The only way to increase military spending by the Federal government is to cut spending on social programs.

(C) Senator Franklin agrees with the policies of his party.

(D) The Orange Party has the majority in the Senate.

(E) Senator Franklin opposes Federal spending on social programs.

Important Strategy

What is the underlying assumption in this example? Note that what you are interested in is the major assumption in the argument—the unstated premise without which the argument wouldn't work.

To make it easier to see how the author proceeds from the premises to the conclusion and to see which premise isn't explicitly stated, you can rewrite the argument as follows, clearly identifying the premises and the conclusion:

> Premise: The Orange Party supports increased military spending by the Federal government.
>
> Premise: Senator Franklin is a member of the Orange Party.
>
> Conclusion: Senator Franklin will vote for a cut in spending on social programs.

It is evident that the conclusion doesn't follow from the premises. In order for this argument to work, there must be another premise, which is assumed by the author. The most important missing link here is the connection between increased military spending by the Federal government and a reduction in spending on social programs. If you insert a premise that connects the two, the argument works:

> Premise: Senator Franklin is a member of the Orange Party.

Premise: The Orange Party endorses higher government spending on the military.

Assumption: The only way to increase military spending by the Federal government is to cut spending on social programs.

Conclusion: Senator Franklin will vote to cut spending on social programs.

It is a good idea to formulate an answer to the question before considering the answer choices. If you can't identify the major assumption, however, use the answer choices to help you. Take the answer choices one at a time and deny the statements they provide. Then look to see what happens to the argument. If the argument isn't affected, the statement isn't the major assumption. If the argument falls apart or stops making sense, you have found the major assumption.

Look!

Important Strategy

You can test this technique on our example. Choice (A) says that elected officials always support the policies endorsed by their parties. To negate this statement, you would say that elected officials do not always support the policies of their parties. The argument isn't affected by this; Senator Franklin may still vote to cut spending on social programs. Notice that since the argument is specifically about the Orange Party and Senator Franklin, it need not assume anything about parties and elected officials in general.

By denying the statement in choice (B), you get a claim that there are other means of increasing military spending by the Federal government than by cutting spending on social programs. If this is so, the connection between military spending and spending for social programs is broken, and the argument falls apart. The statement in (B), therefore, is the major assumption (as we have stated previously).

*Important
Strategy*

In (C) you are told that Senator Franklin agrees with the policies of his party. At first glance it may appear that the opposite of this statement would undermine the argument. If Senator Franklin doesn't agree with the policies of his party, he won't vote in their favor. However, since the statement in (C) doesn't say anything about military and social-program spending specifically, the argument doesn't rest on it.

Choice (D) states that the Orange Party has the majority in the Senate. Neither this statement nor its opposite affects the argument. Therefore, this isn't a major assumption.

Finally, choice (E) states that Senator Franklin opposes spending on social programs. This choice is tempting since it helps to explain why the Senator would vote to cut spending on social programs. However, it doesn't establish a connection between military and social-program spending. The opposite of the statement doesn't affect the argument. Therefore, the statement in (E) isn't a major assumption.

The logic of an argument largely depends on the validity of its major assumption. For instance, in our example, if the assumption that the only way to increase military spending by the Federal government is to cut spending on social programs is valid, the argument makes sense. However, if there are other ways to increase spending, the argument is shaky.

Strengthening and Weakening Arguments

Questions that ask you to strengthen or weaken an argument play a very important role in the Logical Reasoning section. These questions test your understanding of how arguments work and your ability to reinforce the logic of an argument or to undermine it.

Assumptions are central to strengthening and weakening arguments. As we have said, the validity of the major assumption made in an argument largely determines whether that argument is logical. Therefore, a statement that strengthens an argument supports its major assumption. On the other hand, a statement that weakens an argument undermines its major assumption.

To illustrate this point, let's look at another example:

Some scientists have argued that the effect of dust storms on the surface temperature of Mars reliably predicts a "nuclear winter" on Earth following a nuclear war that would stir up a comparable amount of debris.

Look!

Important Strategy

Which of the following, if true, would tend to most weaken the argument predicting a "nuclear winter"?

(A) A nuclear war is unlikely because all participants would suffer almost total annihilation.

(B) The chances of a nuclear war occurring are likely to decrease as a result of disarmament.

(C) People could survive a "nuclear winter" if they were adequately prepared.

(D) There is no evidence of life on Mars.

(E) There is no water in the atmosphere of Mars, and therefore the effect of dust on surface temperature isn't comparable to the corresponding effect on Earth.

The assumption in this example's argument is that a valid comparison can be made between Earth and Mars. To weaken the argument, therefore, you must look to undermine this assumption.

Choices (A), (B), and (C) are essentially irrelevant since none of them address the major assumption of the argument, the prediction of a "nuclear winter."

Choice (D) makes an implicit distinction between Mars and Earth. The presence of life, however, doesn't really affect the argument.

Bust it!

Choice (E) tells you that the conditions on Mars are different from those on Earth; therefore, the effects of dust in the atmospheres of the two planets would be different. This clearly invalidates the assumption underlying the argument and the argument itself. Therefore, (E) is correct.

Although assumptions appear in a great number of questions, not all arguments employ assumptions in their reasoning. In looking to strengthen or weaken an argument without a major underlying assumption, concentrate on the connection between the evidence and the conclusion. To strengthen an argument, select the answer choice which provides additional evidence for the conclusion. To weaken an argument, look for an alternative conclusion which can be made based on the given evidence.

To better understand how to do this, let's look at another example:

> The rate of violent crime has risen over the last ten years. Some sociologists insist that violence depicted on television is responsible for this trend.

Which of the following, if true, would most strengthen the argument?

(A) Violent criminals have more psychological problems than criminals who are not violent.

(B) Guns are used more than any other weapons in violent crimes.

(C) The stringent rules that regulated the content of television programming were greatly eased 15 years ago, resulting in widespread depictions of graphic violence.

(D) The overcrowding of prisons has resulted in reduced terms for many criminals.

(E) Violent criminals are much more prone to suggestion than people who do not commit crimes.

Bust it!

Since you are asked to strengthen the argument in this example, you need to find evidence to support the connection between violent crime and violence depicted on television. You can immediately eliminate choices (A) and (B). Although both (A) and (B) are most likely true, the choices are irrelevant to the argument. You can also eliminate (D) since it weakens the argument. Releasing criminals before they finish their term can be viewed as the reason for an increase in violent crime in the last ten years.

Of the remaining two choices, (C) provides evidence that supports the conclusion. The easing of regulations 15 years ago led to more violence being depicted on television. For the past ten years, there has been an increase in violent crime. The correlation between these events supports the conclusion that depictions of violence on television lead to increases in violent crime.

Choice (E) may be interpreted as providing evidence to support the argument. If violent criminals are more prone to suggestion than noncriminals, they are probably more affected by violence on television. However, to reach this conclusion you have to assume that there is a connection between being prone to suggestion and being affected by television. You can't make such an assumption based on the information in (E). Therefore, (E) doesn't strengthen the argument. Choice (C) is your correct answer.

Methods of Argument

Important Information!

Although you won't be asked to identify any method of argument by name, it is important that you become familiar with some of the more common methods. However, being able to identify different methods and knowing the types of logical errors that are likely to occur in each will help you evaluate arguments.

Deductive Arguments

Deductive arguments are designed to prove definitively the author's conclusion. In a deductive argument, the conclusion necessarily follows from the premises. If the premises are true, the conclusion *must* be true. Deductive arguments use generalizations as premises to prove specific conclusions.

> Premise: All children like chocolate.
>
> Conclusion: My nephew Nick, who is four years old, must like chocolate.

The example above is a valid deductive argument. The conclusion follows necessarily from the premise: If all children like chocolate, my nephew must like chocolate. The argument is valid but untrue—it is unsound—because the premise is false.

Inductive Arguments

Inductive arguments use limited specific experience to support the probability of a generalized conclusion. In an inductive argument, if the premises are true, the conclusion is *probably* true.

Important Information!

Premise:　Tom's stereo has worked every time he has used it.

Conclusion:　Tom's stereo will work today.

In the example above, the conclusion doesn't follow from the premise. The argument is a relatively strong one, however, since the conclusion is probably true if the premise is true.

Causal Arguments

Causal arguments usually appear in explanations. An example of a causal argument is a scientific hypothesis that explains a natural event, e.g., lower global temperatures result from increased volcanic activity.

Important Information!

Quite often, causal arguments confuse correlation—coincidental occurrence—and causality. Do not assume that if *X* happened right before *Y*, *X* caused *Y*. Always consider alternative causes.

Statistical Arguments

Statistical arguments use numerical data in their premises to support an argument.

Premise:　Four out of five dentists recommend Superdent toothpaste to their patients.

Conclusion:　Use Superdent.

Important Information!

Statistical arguments are often invalid because they use samples that are too small or are not representative of the group the conclusion focuses on. Be especially wary of arguments that make conclusions about the whole based on the attributes of its parts, or vice versa.

Analogous Arguments

Important Information!

Analogous arguments use comparisons in their premises.

Premise: Broccoli has been shown to be very beneficial to one's health.

Conclusion: Spinach must also be good for you.

The strength of analogous arguments depends on the similarity between the elements of their analogies. These arguments can never prove their conclusions; they can only support them.

The Two Types of Logical Reasoning Questions

Type 1: PARALLEL REASONING QUESTIONS

Important Information!

Parallel reasoning questions most directly test your grasp of different methods of argument. These questions follow one basic format. An argument is presented to you, and then you are asked to select an argument that uses similar logic.

You have to be careful to select arguments that parallel as closely as possible the ones given in the question. For instance, if the argument in the question is an unsound deductive argument (one whose premises are not true), you have to select the answer choice which also presents an unsound deductive argument. In other words, answers to parallel reasoning questions should reflect the argument completely, including logical flaws.

Here's an example of a parallel reasoning type of question:

Students who do well in sciences must also do well in mathematics. If they did not do well in mathematics, they would not do well in sciences.

Which of the following is logically most similar to the argument above?

(A) **John received straight A's in math, chemistry, biology, and physics. People who do well in math must also do well in sciences.**

(B) **Baseball pitchers who injure their arms must retire. If they do not retire, they may be in danger of a permanent injury.**

(C) **Nine out of ten high-school dropouts find it difficult to support themselves. A diploma increases one's earning potential.**

(D) **Government must act to protect the environment. If the environment isn't protected, the ecosystem will be irrevocably damaged.**

(E) **Criminals must have a history of antisocial behavior. If they were not antisocial, they would not have turned to crime.**

To answer the question in this example, you must first identify the method of argument used. If you look carefully at the argument, however, you will notice that it is impossible to tell which of the two statements is the conclusion, and which is the premise. In fact, both statements say essentially the same thing. This is an example of **circular reasoning.**

Bust it!

You must, therefore, look for an answer choice that presents a circular argument. Choice (A) presents a weak inductive argument. Choice (B) presents an unsound deductive argument. In (C) you have a statistical argument. Choice (D) presents an invalid deductive argument. And, finally, choice (E) presents a circular argument. So choice (E) is your correct answer.

Type 2: INFERENCE QUESTIONS

The second group of Logical Reasoning questions are comprised of several varieties of questions that ask you to draw inferences from given information. These questions are usually worded in one of the following ways:

*Important
Information!*

— Which of the following can be inferred from the passage?

— Which of the following conclusions can most properly be drawn from the passage?

— If the above information is true, which of the following must also be true?

— If the above statements are true, which of the following is probably also true?

Notice that these questions focus on the connection between the premises and the conclusion. Pay particular attention to whether the question asks for the conclusion that must be true or the one that is probably true. Remember the difference between deductive and inductive arguments. Do not insert your own knowledge. And most importantly, do not make assumptions.

Let's do an example:

Ron earns less than Betsy.

Susan and Betsy earn the same amount.

Howard earns more than Susan.

Peter earns more than Ron.

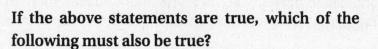

Bust it!

If the above statements are true, which of the following must also be true?

(A) Peter earns more than Susan.

(B) Peter earns more than Howard.

(C) Betsy earns less than Peter.

(D) Susan earns less than Ron.

(E) Howard earns more than Ron.

The question in this example asks which of the statements must be true. In other words, you have to find the statement that necessarily follows from the given information.

To make things clearer, you can symbolize the information (like you did for Analytical Reasoning questions). Below are the four original statements in mathematical notation.

R < B

B = S

S < H

R < P

You can derive further information from these four statements. If Betsy and Susan earn the same amount, and if Betsy earns more than Ron, then Susan also earns more than Ron.

R < S

We also know since Susan and Betsy earn the same amount and if Howard earns more than Susan, then Howard earns more than Betsy.

B < H

If Howard earns more than Betsy, and if Betsy earns more than Ron, then Howard also earns more than Ron.

R < H

Choices (A), (B), and (C) are incorrect. We know that Peter earns more than Ron, but that is all we are given. We do not know if Peter earns more or less than Susan, Howard, or Betsy.

The statement in (D) asserts that Betsy earns less than Ron. You know that this is wrong from the additional information you derived from the original statements.

Choice (E) states that Howard earns more than Ron. Again, from the additional information you derived, you know that this must be true. This statement follows necessarily from the given information. Therefore, the correct answer is (E).

Points to Remember

✔ Logical Reasoning questions focus on specific skills, such as analyzing arguments, recognizing assumptions, drawing inferences, strengthening or weakening arguments, and evaluating the logic of arguments. The questions are designed to test your ability to understand the point the author tries to prove, to see what evidence the author uses to support the conclusion, to trace how the author gets from the evidence to the conclusion, and to judge the effectiveness of the argument.

✔ The first skill you need to practice for Logical Reasoning questions is identifying the conclusions and premises of arguments.

✔ In an argument, an assumption is a premise that isn't explicitly (directly) stated. These unstated premises are very important since the validity of an argument is determined by the validity of its assumptions. In other words, weaken an assumption and you can weaken the argument, and vice-versa.

✔ It is a good idea to formulate an answer to the question before considering the answer choices. If you can't identify the major assumption, however, use the answer choices to help you. Take the answer choices one at a time and deny the statements they provide. Then look to see what happens to the argument. If the argument isn't affected, the statement isn't the major assumption. If the argument falls apart or stops making sense, you have found the major assumption.

On Target!

On Target!

✔   A statement that strengthens an argument supports its major assumption. On the other hand, a statement that weakens an argument undermines its major assumption.

✔   To strengthen an argument, select the answer choice which provides additional evidence for the conclusion. To weaken an argument, look for an alternative conclusion which can be made based on the given evidence.

✔   Although you won't be asked to identify any method of argument by name, it is important that you become familiar with some of the more common methods. But being able to identify different methods and knowing the types of logical errors that are likely to occur in each will help you evaluate arguments.

Drill: Logical Reasoning

1. People who have worked in a large textile mill have recently had their hearing tested. The tests show that one-quarter of the adults suffered from abnormal hearing loss. Hearing loss can occur from loud noise and prolonged exposure to elevated sound levels. Increased age normally results in hearing loss.

Which one of the following would be the most useful information in determining whether the noise from the textile mill is responsible for the hearing loss?

(A) Are the adults older than a typical sample of adults in the general population?
(B) What effects have people who worked in other textile mills reported?
(C) Have those who clean the floors during work hours also developed hearing loss?
(D) What are the long-term effects of impaired hearing?
(E) To what extent have people in other occupations suffered hearing loss?

2. All animal lovers are caring. Barb and Bub opposed each other in the Senate race. Only animal haters voted for Barb. Carl voted for Bub for Senate.

Assuming the statements above are true, which of the following statements lead to contradictions?

I. If Bub is an animal lover, Carl is an animal hater.
II. If Carl is an animal lover, he voted for Barb.
III. Some animal lovers voted for Barb.

(A) I only.
(B) II only.
(C) II and III only.
(D) III only.
(E) I, II, and III.

3. Jelly: Everyone recognizes that Telly is an excellent dancer.

Nelly: Telly is a member of the Dance Show. That must mean that the Dance Show is composed of excellent dancers.

Which one of the following, if true, would contradict Nelly's assumption?

(A) Individual members of an organization are rarely influenced by the characteristics of the organization they join.
(B) Individuals may have a characteristic that the organization does not have.
(C) Individuals tend to seek those who have similar talents.
(D) The sum of the parts is not necessarily less than that of the whole.
(E) An organization tends to take on the characteristics of the individuals.

Questions 4 and 5 refer to the following:

The garbage collector will not win the job of mayor. Still her running for office will be a help. No one else—even experienced candidates—has announced their candidacy. Could the garbage collector open up the race? Anyone who wishes to oppose the current mayor may see the garbage collector's running as _____.

4. The best answer for the blank is

(A) unwanted competition.
(B) an open invitation to run.
(C) a paradigm for a campaign.
(D) unimportant.
(E) a challenge.

5. One can infer that the garbage collector is

(A) "unknown."
(B) likely to split the voters who vote against the mayor.
(C) likely to be the only other candidate.
(D) going to win.
(E) unlikely to affect the campaign.

6. An advertisement I saw in the journal said that more doctors recommend Brand aspirin for their patients who use aspirin. If that is true, Brand aspirin is preferred by most doctors for their patients who use aspirin.

Which one of the following objections is the strongest objection to the conclusion?

(A) Not all patients use aspirin.
(B) Doctors should not recommend any brand of aspirin since aspirin may thin the blood.
(C) Some doctors do not recommend Brand aspirin for their patients who use aspirin.
(D) The phrase "more doctors recommend Brand aspirin for their patients who use aspirin" is too ambiguous to provide support for the author's conclusion.
(E) Doctors are not the best qualified persons to judge which aspirin their patients should use.

7. Since our state had a particularly warm winter last year, our capital city probably had a particularly warm winter last year.

Which argument below most closely simulates the argument above?

(A) Since we have had below average rainfall on our ranch, our area was probably dry during the past year.
(B) Since vegetable prices are up, lettuce and cabbage are probably high.
(C) Since rainfall is necessary for the production of grain, this year we will probably have a good harvest.
(D) Since I develop hives from oranges, I will decline the orange juice.
(E) Since the wheat harvest was down this year, the barley harvest will also be down.

Questions 8 and 9 refer to the following:

Learning modalities are of several different types. Some people learn best by doing. Others learn best by hearing. Still others learn best by seeing. One's learning modalities _____.

8. Which one of the following best completes the sentence?

(A) are unimportant since students must adjust to the teacher.
(B) could be important for a teacher to know.
(C) cannot be determined.
(D) should not modify the curriculum.
(E) is a mystery to the learner—even as an adult.

9. One can infer that

(A) teachers cannot accommodate their students.
(B) students must adapt to their teachers, not teachers to their classes.
(C) a teacher should consider the styles or modality of the learner.
(D) students must adapt to the subject, not the subject to the student.
(E) learning styles can never change.

10. If June's teacher does not support June's research efforts, June will probably change the research topic.

Logically, if June's teacher does support June's research efforts, June

(A) will lose faith in her research project.
(B) may or may not lose faith in her project.
(C) will definitely not change the topic she is pursuing.
(D) will probably not continue the research.
(E) will probably pursue a different research effort than the one she has begun.

11. Americans often consider themselves as open-minded and willing to consider new ideas. It seems paradoxical that, with regard to the metric system,

(A) Americans are willing to study and consider changing their system of measurement.
(B) Americans have not had a chance to review and study the system in detail at this time.
(C) Americans will not consider the change to that system.
(D) Americans have found many shortcomings, inconsistencies, and mistakes.
(E) Americans are willing to make a change to the metric system of measurement.

12. Energy conservation groups have called upon citizens to install in their shower heads a device to conserve water. This device does not seem to affect the water pressure, but it does save on water used during a shower and, therefore, on the energy needed to heat this water. The energy conservation groups suggest that these sacrifices on the part of an individual can help society in a small way now and in the future.

The plea from the energy conservation groups is misleading if which one of the following is true?

(A) The shower head device is quite inexpensive.
(B) Most shower heads are designed so as to waste water—especially hot water.
(C) Energy waste is actually caused by large businesses and not by individuals.
(D) The shower head device pays for itself in savings on water and energy bills.
(E) Irrigation consumes more water than households.

13. A recent study shows that those who work hard, who exercise, and who work long hours are often exhausted. Working hard and exercising are dangers to one's health since one's energy level and metabolism can be lowered by hard work. Those who work at a job often do not have the energy for exercise.

Which one of the following, if true, most seriously weakens the study's conclusion?

(A) Bill helped to conduct the study and he is a liar.
(B) Exercise programs on the corporate level for hard workers are often unsupervised.
(C) Energy levels are often higher among those who exercise regularly.
(D) Other studies bear out the problems with low metabolism among those who exercise.
(E) Jim works hard and he, too, is tired.

14. Students in a ceramics class have had some of their clay pieces explode when they attempted to fire or bake this green ware. Their teacher tells them that such explosion of their products can occur in several situations. If air bubbles remain in the clay that the students mold by hand or in the slip (liquid clay) that they pour into the molds, the air will expand when the temperature increases and the green ware may break. Pieces which are not thoroughly dried or cured may break when fired because the moisture expands as the temperature rises. If a piece is glazed or painted and the glaze or paint does not dry thoroughly before the students fire the piece, breakage can occur.

If what the teacher says is true and if the green ware is dry before the firing, the breakage must be because

(A) there were air bubbles in the clay.
(B) the paint or glaze was not dry before firing.

(C) a piece was glazed or painted and the glaze or paint did not dry thoroughly before the students fired the piece.
(D) either there were air bubbles in the clay or slip, or the paint or glaze was not dry before firing, or both.
(E) there were air bubbles in the clay or slip, and the paint or glaze was not dry before firing.

15. Which one of the following is an inference one can make from the information about the breaking of items in the kiln?

(A) One cannot prevent breakage when firing green ware.
(B) Pieces which are not thoroughly dried or cured may break when fired because the moisture expands as the temperature rises.
(C) Moisture in the paint or glaze might expand and cause the clay piece to break.
(D) If there are air bubbles in the clay that the students mold by hand or in the slip (liquid clay) that they pour into the molds, the air will expand when the temperature increases and the green ware may break.
(E) If the students glaze or paint a piece and the glaze or paint does not dry thoroughly before the students fire the piece, breakage can occur when the moisture in the paint or glaze expands—especially if the moisture has penetrated the clay.

16. Rudolf Flesch wrote a book titled *Why Johnny Can't Read*. He stated that the reason that many school children in the 1950s and 1960s were reading more poorly than children in the 1930s was that the teachers were using the sight word method. He cited statistics that there were more remedial reading classes in the 1950s and the 1960s than in the 1930s to prove his point. He advocated that parents begin to teach children to read at five—before most started formal schooling—and that the parents use phonics.

Flesch, however, fails to recognize that the schools did not try to educate all children in the 1930s. The dropout rate was higher than in the 1950s and the 1960s. Children who may have had difficulty learning in school did not even attend school in many cases in the 1930s. Not as many classes for remedial students were needed because the remedial reading students were not even in school.

The passage criticizes Flesch's position by

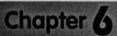

(A) attacking the person rather than his argument.

(B) charging that he assumes correlation where only causation is shown.

(C) showing that the conclusions are merely repetitions of their assumptions.

(D) showing that the arguments rely on an ambiguity in the phrase "sight word method."

(E) reinterpreting the evidence that Flesch used.

17. Manuel: I'm scared that I might develop colon cancer.

Juan: Have no fear, Manuel. Anyone who is under 25 runs a small risk of getting the disease. You are only 18. You have little chance of getting the disease.

Of the following arguments, which one exhibits the same logical flaw as that exhibited in Juan's remark?

(A) Any child who disobeys the teacher must leave the room. If you are a child who disobeys the teacher, you will be forced to leave the room.

(B) Any new recruit who cannot pass the eye test cannot fly a plane. If you can pass the eye test, you can get your pilot's license.

(C) If your weight is high, your chances for high blood pressure are high. Your weight is about right. You probably do not have high blood pressure.

(D) Anyone who scores high on the SAT and has a high grade point average is eligible to enter Learning College. You have a high grade point average so you are eligible to enter Learning College.

(E) Any bookstore that sells my novel, but not my biography, is not worthy of my patronage. So if the bookstore sells my novel and my biography, it is worthy of my patronage.

18. The National Wildlife Service is making my life miserable. It tells me when I can hunt game and when I can't. It tells me what I can hunt and what I can't. Next, NWS makes me buy a license to fish. When I lived in the country, I could fish in my pond when I wanted to do so. Now I have to pay to fish at an ocean nobody owns. What's next? A rule telling me what kind of rod and reel I can use?

Which one of the following statements best expresses the speaker's central point?

(A) The right to fish, once given, should not require a fishing license.

(B) It is unreasonable for the National Wildlife Service to decide for individuals when to hunt and what to hunt.

(C) A hunter ought to have a choice to hunt game when he or she wants.

(D) The National Wildlife Service ought not to over-legislate.

(E) The National Wildlife Service ought not to over-legislate with regard to hunting and fishing.

19. In a classroom, the students must obey the rules of the school. This means that the teacher must enforce the rules in her classroom. What does the speaker assume?

(A) That the teacher is a first-year teacher.

(B) That the rules are posted or made known.

(C) That the teacher knows the rules.

(D) That the rules are just.

(E) That the principal set up the rules.

20. One of the following is an invalid argument. Which one is it?

(A) If Jane goes, then Bill goes.
Not Jane.
Therefore, not Bill.

(B) Only if Jane goes, then Bill goes.
Not Jane.
Therefore, Bill.

(C) If Jane goes, then Bill goes.
Therefore, if Bill,
either Bill only or both Jane and Bill.

(D) If Jane goes, then Bill goes.
Bill does not go.
Therefore, Jane does not go.

(E) Either Jane or Bill goes but not both.
Bill does not go.
Therefore, Jane goes.

21. Which one of the following is invalid?

(A) If Smew is a lawyer, then he passed the bar.
Smew did not pass the bar.
Therefore, Smew is not a lawyer.

(B) If Smew is a lawyer, then he passed the bar.
Therefore, if Smew passed the bar, he is a lawyer.

   (C) If Smew passed the bar, then he can be a
       lawyer.
       Therefore, if Smew did not pass the bar, he
       cannot be a lawyer.
   (D) If Smew is a lawyer, then he passed the bar.
       Smew is now a lawyer.
       Smew passed the bar.
   (E) If you are a lawyer, then you passed the bar.
       Smew is a lawyer.
       Therefore, he passed the bar.

22. Mary Jane was able to drop 20 points in her cholesterol profile in only six months. She should be able to have her cholesterol in the normal range by New Year's Day.

This argument may be invalid because of

(A) the strength of the argument.
(B) circular reasoning.
(C) cause and effect.
(D) the fact that it is an *ad hominem* argument.
(E) the fact that it is an analogy.

23. Barbara's spelling grades improved 100% when the teacher switched to the new spelling books. Therefore, we know that the new books are best for our child.

Which one of the following, if true, would most seriously weaken the author's conclusion?

(A) Statistics show that over 3,000 children have higher test scores after using the books.
(B) The number of people who use the books is over 30,000.
(C) More than 30 states have used the book.
(D) Barbara only got one word right on her test in the other spelling book; she got two words right on this spelling test—a 100% improvement.
(E) The University of Good Faith is performing further studies.

24. Benet: I am sure that our teacher, Mrs. Jones, has written a new book.

Monet: I work at the local bookstore and I know of no new book by Mrs. Jones.

The method of persuasion in Monet's argument is

(A) analogy.   (D) generalization.
(B) omission.   (E) cause and effect.
(C) appeal to ignorance.

25. We have had two student teachers from Old Joe College. Both were good workers. We'll take all the student teachers Old Joe College wants to send us.

This argument is an example of

(A) analogy.   (D) generalization.
(B) omission.   (E) cause and effect.
(C) appeal to ignorance.

26. I was wearing this sweater when our high school team won the tournament. I am going to wear this sweater to take my final exams.

This argument is an example of

(A) causal.
(B) omission.
(C) appeal to ignorance.
(D) analogy.
(E) circular reasoning.

27. Students who read well read a lot. I read well; therefore, I must read a lot. To read a lot, you must read well. To read well, you must read a lot.

This argument is an example of

(A) causal.
(B) omission.
(C) appeal to ignorance.
(D) analogy.
(E) circular reasoning.

28. Brad: Jim is running for public office. He should not be elected, however, since he is a cheat.

The above argument is an example of

(A) causal.
(B) omission.
(C) appeal to ignorance.
(D) *ad hominem*.
(E) circular reasoning.

29. We phoned everybody in the small town at their residence at 10 a.m. on Tuesday. We found that those we talked with would vote for Jim Smith, not Joe Jones.

The argument above depends on which one of the following assumptions?

(A) People at home at 10 a.m. are typical of the population of the small town.
(B) People with telephones are typical of the population of the town.
(C) People at home at 10 a.m. and with telephones are representative of the small town.
(D) Each of the persons who made the calls was personable.
(E) Each of the persons on the telephone was a registered voter.

30. Margie: George Smith is too young to run for political office, is not a U.S. citizen, and is an alcoholic.

    Charlie: George Smith is actually 45 years old and has been a U.S. citizen all his life.

    The above argument is an example of

    (A) causal.
    (B) omission.
    (C) appeal to ignorance.
    (D) *ad hominem.*
    (E) circular reasoning.

31. Jen: Mary has missed three days on the job. She does not care to do her work well.

    Ben: Mary has had to take care of her family. She is using the Family Leave Act to cover these absences.

    The above argument is an example of

    (A) causal.
    (B) omission.
    (C) appeal to ignorance.
    (D) *ad hominem.*
    (E) using an alternative explanation.

32. Which one of the arguments below is an example of recognizing that the argument makes the logical fallacy, "*post hoc, ergo propter hoc*"?

    (A) "I don't believe that Mark is competent as an administrator. I have known him for three years and I have never seen him make a decision on his own."
    (B) "You say that the new product is costly, difficult to make, and ugly. I find that it is less expensive than the one we make now and will be easy to make on our new forms."

(C) "I found that studying with the radio on helps me concentrate. I know. I studied with the radio on before my last algebra exam and I made a good grade."
(D) "I saw three boys on Hayne Street after midnight. That is a neighborhood that does not care for its young."
(E) "If you drop out of school, it will be difficult for you to help your children with their homework. The children might then drop out of school and they will be unable to help their children with homework."

33. Joan: I know that I can dance well. I am certain that I am one of the best dancers in the room. I am going dancing regularly.

    Joan makes which one of the following mistakes in the passage above?

    (A) She cites an example to prove a point.
    (B) She assumes that event *A* caused event *B* simply because *A* preceded *B*.
    (C) She identifies a contradiction.
    (D) She reiterates her conclusion rather than supplying evidence to support it.
    (E) She misinterprets the meaning of the words "going dancing."

34. Bronta: Old College has an excellent technical preparation program. Billy went there. You know how competent he is.

    Bronta makes which one of the following mistakes in the passage above?

    (A) She cites an example to prove a point.
    (B) She assumes that event *B* caused event *A* simply because *B* preceded *A.*
    (C) She identifies a contradiction.
    (D) She reiterates her conclusion rather than supplying evidence to support it.
    (E) She misinterprets the meaning of the words "technical preparation."

35. Jimmie: Your work is totally unsatisfactory. You must be a better worker to keep your job.

    Jimmie's statement is a good example of which one of the following?

    (A) Causal   (D) *Ad hominem*
    (B) Inconsistency   (E) Ambiguity
    (C) Appeal to ignorance

36. "I am determined to save money. I went to the sale and purchased a new fall wardrobe. I must have saved more than $50 by buying these new clothes."

    This statement is a good example of which one of the following?

    (A) Causal
    (B) Inconsistency
    (C) Appeal to ignorance
    (D) *Ad hominem*
    (E) Ambiguity

37. Bill: Democrats are liberals. I would never vote for one.

    John: Sam is very conservative. He does not support government subsidies or any kind of government grants.

    John's statement is a good example of which one of the following?

    (A) Causal
    (B) Inconsistency
    (C) Counter-example
    (D) *Ad hominem*
    (E) Ambiguity

38. Bryan: I understand that there was some trouble on the work floor. As your supervisor, I need to know if there was actually an attack.

    Shawn: I wonder if the new man you hired is actually from the South?

    Shawn's statement is a good example of which one of the following?

    (A) Causal
    (B) Diverting the issue
    (C) Counter-example
    (D) *Ad hominem*
    (E) Ambiguity

39. The latest study indicates that students who use the new Read With Meaning Program have a higher rate of comprehension than do students who do not use the program, lending support to the view that lack of use of the program contributes to poor comprehension.

    The argument would be weakened most by pointing out which one of the following?

    (A) Statistics can be deceiving.
    (B) Many genetic backgrounds were represented in both the program group and the non-program group.
    (C) Participants in the study were chosen at random from a larger population.
    (D) Some children who did not use the program had higher rates of comprehension than did students who did use the program.
    (E) Many variables, such as age, intelligence, and years in school, were not accounted for in the study.

40. Using an artificial sweetener poses none of the risks of the use of sugar as a sweetener. An artificial sweetener does not cause a weight gain. It does not aggravate diabetes or contribute to dental cavities. Therefore, we should encourage the use of artificial sweeteners—especially for young children.

    Which one of the following statements, if true, most seriously weakens the argument for the use of artificial sweeteners?

    (A) There have been very few studies on the cost effectiveness of artificial sweeteners.
    (B) Companies producing artificial sweetener have usually conducted the studies of the safety of artificial sweeteners.
    (C) Using artificial sweeteners would reduce the grocery bills of most families.
    (D) The cost of dental services is extremely high for the victims of dental cavities.
    (E) There are long-term health risks to using artificial sweeteners.

Logical Reasoning Drill
ANSWER KEY

1. (E)	21. (B)
2. (C)	22. (A)
3. (B)	23. (D)
4. (B)	24. (C)
5. (A)	25. (D)
6. (D)	26. (A)
7. (B)	27. (E)
8. (B)	28. (D)
9. (C)	29. (C)
10. (B)	30. (B)
11. (C)	31. (E)
12. (D)	32. (C)
13. (C)	33. (D)
14. (D)	34. (A)
15. (E)	35. (E)
16. (E)	36. (B)
17. (C)	37. (C)
18. (E)	38. (B)
19. (D)	39. (E)
20. (A)	40. (E)

Attacking the Writing Sample

In addition to the three types of multiple-choice questions on the LSAT, there is a 30-minute essay on an assigned topic. The Writing Sample will always appear at the end of the LSAT; therefore, you—and all the other test-takers—will complete the essay at a time when you are probably already tired! Your careful preparation for this portion will help you to write a persuasive—if not perfect—essay for the LSAT.

Important Information!

There are always three parts to the writing section.

1.   **You will be provided with a brief introduction that outlines the topic of the essay.**

2.   **You must base your decision on set criteria.**

3.   **You will have two—always two—options from which you must choose.**

Important Information!

It is extremely important that you understand that you will not receive a score for the Writing Section. Instead, each law school which receives your score report will also be given an unmarked photocopy of your Writing Sample. Each law school decides how—or if—it will use this essay during its admissions process. **Yes, it is possible that no one will ever read your Writing Sample!** Law schools are primarily interested in your LSAT score and your GPA.

After reading this, you may ask yourself why you should even bother studying for the Writing Sample. Good question! Our advice is to study for the scored sections of the LSAT (Reading Comprehension, Logical Reasoning, and Analytical Reasoning), and once you feel comfortable with those areas, THEN study this chapter. If you find you are running out of time before your test day, ignore the Writing Sample and concentrate on the scored areas.

The Directions

There are three main parts to the Writing Section of the LSAT:

Important Information!

1. An **opening statement**, which will present the information.

2. The **guidelines**, which you will use as a basis in presenting your argument.

3. The two **choices**, from which you select **one option**.

You should make sure you study the directions for the Writing Section of the LSAT so that you do not have to waste part of your 30 minutes trying to determine your task. The directions will appear as follows:

> <u>**DIRECTIONS**</u>: You have 30 minutes in which to plan and write the brief writing exercise on the topic below. Read the topic carefully. You will probably find it best to spend a few minutes considering the topic and organizing your thoughts before you begin writing. **Do not write on a topic other than the one specified. Writing on a topic of your own choice is not acceptable.**
>
> There is no "right" or "wrong" position on this topic. Law schools are interested in how skillfully you support the position you take and how clearly you express that position. How well you write is much more important than how much you write. No special knowledge is required or expected. Law schools are interested in organization, vocabulary, and writing mechanics. They understand the short time available to you and the pressure under which you are writing.
>
> Confine your writing to the lined area inside the booklet. Only the blocked line area will be reproduced for the law schools. You will find that you have enough space if you plan your writing carefully, write on every line, avoid wide margins, and keep your handwriting a reasonable size. Be sure that your handwriting is legible.
>
> The writing sample is photocopied and sent to law schools to which you direct your LSAT score. Use only the pen provided at the test center to complete the writing sample; this will ensure a photocopy of high quality. (Pens are *not* used on the computerized answer sheet; this requires a No. 2 pencil.)

Important Information!

Expectations

You need to consider the expectations for you on this part of the LSAT:

Important Information!

1) You may not take any paper with you into the testing site. From the test administrator or test proctor, you will receive paper, pen, and a writing sample booklet for the essay portion.

2) The main purpose of the section is for you to write a logical, concise, persuasive argument which supports your position on the issue.

3) The law schools and test examiners do not expect you to have a knowledge of the law or legal matters to write the essay.

4) You must base your argument on the information provided.

5) You will have only 30 minutes to:

   a. review the facts,

   b. pick a clear position to defend,

   c. support your position effectively and persuasively,

   d. write within the framework of the provided information, and

   e. attack opposing views, arguments, and facts.

6) You must address all of the main points in the information provided.

Important Information!

7) You should realize that there is no correct choice in the two options. You should simply choose the option with which you are most able to respond.

8) Do not include any criteria other than those in the topic.

About the Writing Sample

Your first step is to analyze the writing topic. Outline your response by identifying:

1. your position and two arguments in favor of your position,

2. the rejected position and two arguments in favor of that position, and

3. the weak points in your position and the weak points in the other position.

Important Information!

You are now ready to write your essay. There are two main ways to construct your four-paragraph argument or essay.

Form I:
Paragraph one

This introductory paragraph explains your position and two arguments for your position. (Consider starting with the words *although* or *while* so you can acknowledge that there is another point of view and a weakness to your position.)

Paragraph two

This paragraph presents reason one for your argument and explains that the other choice does not have this supporting criteria. Present your best argument first.

Paragraph three

This paragraph presents the other option and two arguments against the choice.

Paragraph four

This conclusion restates your choice and your reasoning in two or three sentences. You should not repeat yourself exactly. The paragraph ends with a strong sentence which concisely reaffirms your position.

Form II:
Paragraph one

This introductory paragraph explains your position and two arguments for your position. (Consider starting with the words *although* or *while* so you can acknowledge that there is another point of view and a weakness to your position.)

Paragraph two

This paragraph presents your choice and two arguments in favor of the choice. (You should present your best argument first.)

Paragraph three

This paragraph presents reason two for your argument and explains that the other choice does not have this supporting criteria.

Paragraph four

The concluding paragraph restates your position and the reasoning behind this choice without repeating yourself. You should end with a strong sentence that concisely reaffirms your position.

Tips for Writing Your Persuasive Argument

- **Tip 1:**   *Make sure all your handwriting is legible. Neatness is important!*

- **Tip 2:**   *Choose a position immediately, without regard to your personal biases. Do not waste time with personal morals, ethics, or political convictions.*

- **Tip 3:**   *In your essay, use terms and phrases from the guidelines and from the situations you have chosen.*

- **Tip 4:**   *Outline your essay ideas on scrap paper. Make sure your ideas are organized.*

Look!

Important Strategy

Look!

**Important
Strategy**

- **Tip 5:**   *For each sentence, think about sentence structure—then write.*

- **Tip 6:**   *Avoid "I" and "we" throughout your essay. The third person approach will help focus your thoughts on the assignment.*

- **Tip 7:**   *Be concise and specific. Omit wordy expressions. More is not necessarily better!*

Wordy (and Passive)	**Concise**
It is believed that...	*I believe that...*
It should be noted that...	*Notice that...*

- **Tip 8:**   *Substitute a different word for any that you cannot spell. It is better to use a smaller word and spell it correctly than to use a larger, misspelled word.*

- **Tip 9:**   *Keep track of the time as you work!*

- **Tip 10:**   *Review your writing and mechanics skills, if you need to do so, in an English grammar book, before the exam.*

- **Tip 11:**   *Make your corrections neatly! To add a word, use the caret (^). To add a whole*

Look!

Important Strategy

section, make a note in the paper where the insertion should come and write the section at the end. To delete a word, make one mark though the word. To delete a paragraph, make a large X through the paragraph; this is quicker and neater than scratching out each word.

• **Tip 12 :**   Avoid slang, "intellectual" jargon, and "in" words or phrases. Keep it simple. Contradictions and cliches also do not work well informal writing.

• **Tip 13 :**   To clarify the expression of your reasoning, use words like "since", "because", "although", "therefore", "thus", and "however" to introduce statements.

Points to Remember

Point 1: Review the guidelines presented for your consideration. Then read the situation you have chosen.

Point 2: Write with deliberate speed, but be sure to write legibly. Remember if your essay cannot be read, it cannot be graded.

Point 3: Keep your sentences relatively short and in control.

Point 4: The basic structure of your essay should include an introduction, an argument, and a conclusion.

Point 5: Omit wordy expressions.

On Target!

Point 6: Substitute a different word for any that you cannot spell.

Point 7: Plan your essay within the parameters of the allotted time.

Point 8: Review your writing and mechanics skills if you need to do so.

Point 9: Make your corrections neatly!

Drill: Writing Sample

Sample Topic

The following is an example of the type of Writing Sample Topic that will appear on the LSAT. It has been labelled for this drill, so that you can easily recognize and analyze each of the different parts of the topic.

(Opening Statement)

Write an argument in support of a national newspaper's decision to run one of the following two stories. Since both are based on controversial issues, the following considerations should guide your decision:

(Guidelines)

• Although a person has certain rights to privacy, the public also has a right to know certain information which may be important for them to know.

• Freedom of the press is guaranteed by the First Amendment to the Constitution of the United States.

(Situations)

In the first story, the newspaper *The U.S. Ledger* has decided to publicize the name of a rape victim, although all other news media have not publicized the name due to a respect for the victim's privacy. However, the suspected rapist's name was publicized by all media from the moment the event became public knowledge. The victim is now suffering from extreme anxiety due to the knowledge that her name was released as the victim of a rape, although she was assured by the police that all information would be kept confidential. A point was also made in regard to the suspected rapist's right to privacy. His name was made public although, in the eyes of the law, he is innocent until proven guilty. Publicizing him as a "suspected" rapist has cast a shadow on his reputation even though he may be found innocent.

In the second story, the newspaper *The U.S. Ledger* has decided to print a scandalous story about a well-known governor. As soon as the story is run, the governor's career will most likely be ruined. According to the story, long before the governor entered politics he was involved in an attempt to buy a baby through the black market. The incident reportedly began when his wife informed him that she could not have children. Those involved in the black market operated through connections in hospitals. Reports say that doctors would perform unnecessary caesarian sections on expectant mothers and then inform the mothers that their children were stillborn. In the meantime, the baby would be removed from the hospital and sold on the black market to the highest bidder. Sources say that the governor had prior knowledge as to what would be involved in obtaining a baby. The governor's attempt to buy a child was unsuccessful due to complications with the newborn child.

A Writing Sample

(Introduction)

In an increasingly wide-ranging media-centered world, the unveiling of people's private lives has become a lucrative yet sensationalistic obsession. Often times, an individual's right to privacy will be breached at the cost of his or her dignity solely for the entertainment of the public, whose lives and personal rights are usually unaffected by the secret. Sensationalism in media, however, does have practical informational benefits for society, at times—not to mention that it is protected by the First Amendment right to freedom of the press. A secret that goes on without discovery can influence other members of society who may be unaware of its effects. Whether or not the governor is guilty of this illegal action in the case above, a breech of his right to privacy could yield valuable information about some dangerous societal secrets in which the rights of innocent others are violated. A close consideration of the above points about people's rights should prove the newspaper's decision to be within the boundaries of responsible journalism.

(Argument)

The first consideration mentions that people have certain rights to privacy. While this is a legitimate fact, the governor's right to privacy can perpetuate the stealing of babies out of the womb, a serious infringement upon the human rights of innocent mothers-to-be, not to mention families-to-be. If the governor's secret remains untold, the rights of the victimized women and families may continue being violated. In addition, the first consideration also mentions that among people's rights is "the right to know certain information which may be important for them to know." This is precisely where the media can help. Publicity of the governor's secret will inform victims and potential victims of the existence and methods of the black market baby trade. The unveiling of the secret to the public will also inform the people about what such an incident represents about the governor's nature. The public should know if they have put a man in office who is susceptible to such ruthless and illegal behavior as buying babies out of the womb.

The second consideration has to do with the freedom of the press and its implications. The scandalous nature of the story may mean it is untrue. But, in printing such a story, *The U.S. Ledger* is putting its own authority and reputation on the line. In such a sensationalistic case of defamation, the newspaper had better be accurate about its facts, otherwise, it will lose credibility in the public eye. On the other hand, if the paper is indeed the first medium to provide the public with this information, it has provided a public service in alerting the public to both the black market baby trade and the questionable nature of the governor. If it is a reliable source of news, the paper's decision to run the story should prove to be good journalism in a free press society.

(Conclusion)

The above considerations thus weighed, it is a good journalistic move to run the scandalous story of the governor. The story is sensationalistic in nature and is also a breech of the governor's right to privacy; however, the governor's own right to privacy is hardly equal to the many individual rights violated by the public's ignorance of the situation. The governor's secret, if and when it is revealed, is one that could be crucial information for many members of society, especially those people who will be affected by the black market baby trade and the people the governor represents in legislation. Journalism can correct the situation by providing this important information.

LSAT Practice Test
Answer Sheet

SECTION 1

1. Ⓐ Ⓑ Ⓒ Ⓓ Ⓔ
2. Ⓐ Ⓑ Ⓒ Ⓓ Ⓔ
3. Ⓐ Ⓑ Ⓒ Ⓓ Ⓔ
4. Ⓐ Ⓑ Ⓒ Ⓓ Ⓔ
5. Ⓐ Ⓑ Ⓒ Ⓓ Ⓔ
6. Ⓐ Ⓑ Ⓒ Ⓓ Ⓔ
7. Ⓐ Ⓑ Ⓒ Ⓓ Ⓔ
8. Ⓐ Ⓑ Ⓒ Ⓓ Ⓔ
9. Ⓐ Ⓑ Ⓒ Ⓓ Ⓔ
10. Ⓐ Ⓑ Ⓒ Ⓓ Ⓔ
11. Ⓐ Ⓑ Ⓒ Ⓓ Ⓔ
12. Ⓐ Ⓑ Ⓒ Ⓓ Ⓔ
13. Ⓐ Ⓑ Ⓒ Ⓓ Ⓔ
14. Ⓐ Ⓑ Ⓒ Ⓓ Ⓔ
15. Ⓐ Ⓑ Ⓒ Ⓓ Ⓔ
16. Ⓐ Ⓑ Ⓒ Ⓓ Ⓔ
17. Ⓐ Ⓑ Ⓒ Ⓓ Ⓔ
18. Ⓐ Ⓑ Ⓒ Ⓓ Ⓔ
19. Ⓐ Ⓑ Ⓒ Ⓓ Ⓔ
20. Ⓐ Ⓑ Ⓒ Ⓓ Ⓔ
21. Ⓐ Ⓑ Ⓒ Ⓓ Ⓔ
22. Ⓐ Ⓑ Ⓒ Ⓓ Ⓔ
23. Ⓐ Ⓑ Ⓒ Ⓓ Ⓔ
24. Ⓐ Ⓑ Ⓒ Ⓓ Ⓔ
25. Ⓐ Ⓑ Ⓒ Ⓓ Ⓔ
26. Ⓐ Ⓑ Ⓒ Ⓓ Ⓔ
27. Ⓐ Ⓑ Ⓒ Ⓓ Ⓔ
28. Ⓐ Ⓑ Ⓒ Ⓓ Ⓔ
29. Ⓐ Ⓑ Ⓒ Ⓓ Ⓔ
30. Ⓐ Ⓑ Ⓒ Ⓓ Ⓔ

SECTION 2

1. Ⓐ Ⓑ Ⓒ Ⓓ Ⓔ
2. Ⓐ Ⓑ Ⓒ Ⓓ Ⓔ
3. Ⓐ Ⓑ Ⓒ Ⓓ Ⓔ
4. Ⓐ Ⓑ Ⓒ Ⓓ Ⓔ
5. Ⓐ Ⓑ Ⓒ Ⓓ Ⓔ
6. Ⓐ Ⓑ Ⓒ Ⓓ Ⓔ
7. Ⓐ Ⓑ Ⓒ Ⓓ Ⓔ
8. Ⓐ Ⓑ Ⓒ Ⓓ Ⓔ
9. Ⓐ Ⓑ Ⓒ Ⓓ Ⓔ
10. Ⓐ Ⓑ Ⓒ Ⓓ Ⓔ
11. Ⓐ Ⓑ Ⓒ Ⓓ Ⓔ
12. Ⓐ Ⓑ Ⓒ Ⓓ Ⓔ
13. Ⓐ Ⓑ Ⓒ Ⓓ Ⓔ
14. Ⓐ Ⓑ Ⓒ Ⓓ Ⓔ
15. Ⓐ Ⓑ Ⓒ Ⓓ Ⓔ
16. Ⓐ Ⓑ Ⓒ Ⓓ Ⓔ
17. Ⓐ Ⓑ Ⓒ Ⓓ Ⓔ
18. Ⓐ Ⓑ Ⓒ Ⓓ Ⓔ
19. Ⓐ Ⓑ Ⓒ Ⓓ Ⓔ
20. Ⓐ Ⓑ Ⓒ Ⓓ Ⓔ
21. Ⓐ Ⓑ Ⓒ Ⓓ Ⓔ
22. Ⓐ Ⓑ Ⓒ Ⓓ Ⓔ
23. Ⓐ Ⓑ Ⓒ Ⓓ Ⓔ
24. Ⓐ Ⓑ Ⓒ Ⓓ Ⓔ
25. Ⓐ Ⓑ Ⓒ Ⓓ Ⓔ
26. Ⓐ Ⓑ Ⓒ Ⓓ Ⓔ
27. Ⓐ Ⓑ Ⓒ Ⓓ Ⓔ
28. Ⓐ Ⓑ Ⓒ Ⓓ Ⓔ
29. Ⓐ Ⓑ Ⓒ Ⓓ Ⓔ
30. Ⓐ Ⓑ Ⓒ Ⓓ Ⓔ

SECTION 3

1. Ⓐ Ⓑ Ⓒ Ⓓ Ⓔ
2. Ⓐ Ⓑ Ⓒ Ⓓ Ⓔ
3. Ⓐ Ⓑ Ⓒ Ⓓ Ⓔ
4. Ⓐ Ⓑ Ⓒ Ⓓ Ⓔ
5. Ⓐ Ⓑ Ⓒ Ⓓ Ⓔ
6. Ⓐ Ⓑ Ⓒ Ⓓ Ⓔ
7. Ⓐ Ⓑ Ⓒ Ⓓ Ⓔ
8. Ⓐ Ⓑ Ⓒ Ⓓ Ⓔ
9. Ⓐ Ⓑ Ⓒ Ⓓ Ⓔ
10. Ⓐ Ⓑ Ⓒ Ⓓ Ⓔ
11. Ⓐ Ⓑ Ⓒ Ⓓ Ⓔ
12. Ⓐ Ⓑ Ⓒ Ⓓ Ⓔ
13. Ⓐ Ⓑ Ⓒ Ⓓ Ⓔ
14. Ⓐ Ⓑ Ⓒ Ⓓ Ⓔ
15. Ⓐ Ⓑ Ⓒ Ⓓ Ⓔ
16. Ⓐ Ⓑ Ⓒ Ⓓ Ⓔ
17. Ⓐ Ⓑ Ⓒ Ⓓ Ⓔ
18. Ⓐ Ⓑ Ⓒ Ⓓ Ⓔ
19. Ⓐ Ⓑ Ⓒ Ⓓ Ⓔ
20. Ⓐ Ⓑ Ⓒ Ⓓ Ⓔ
21. Ⓐ Ⓑ Ⓒ Ⓓ Ⓔ
22. Ⓐ Ⓑ Ⓒ Ⓓ Ⓔ
23. Ⓐ Ⓑ Ⓒ Ⓓ Ⓔ
24. Ⓐ Ⓑ Ⓒ Ⓓ Ⓔ
25. Ⓐ Ⓑ Ⓒ Ⓓ Ⓔ
26. Ⓐ Ⓑ Ⓒ Ⓓ Ⓔ
27. Ⓐ Ⓑ Ⓒ Ⓓ Ⓔ
28. Ⓐ Ⓑ Ⓒ Ⓓ Ⓔ
29. Ⓐ Ⓑ Ⓒ Ⓓ Ⓔ
30. Ⓐ Ⓑ Ⓒ Ⓓ Ⓔ

SECTION 4

1. Ⓐ Ⓑ Ⓒ Ⓓ Ⓔ
2. Ⓐ Ⓑ Ⓒ Ⓓ Ⓔ
3. Ⓐ Ⓑ Ⓒ Ⓓ Ⓔ
4. Ⓐ Ⓑ Ⓒ Ⓓ Ⓔ
5. Ⓐ Ⓑ Ⓒ Ⓓ Ⓔ
6. Ⓐ Ⓑ Ⓒ Ⓓ Ⓔ
7. Ⓐ Ⓑ Ⓒ Ⓓ Ⓔ
8. Ⓐ Ⓑ Ⓒ Ⓓ Ⓔ
9. Ⓐ Ⓑ Ⓒ Ⓓ Ⓔ
10. Ⓐ Ⓑ Ⓒ Ⓓ Ⓔ
11. Ⓐ Ⓑ Ⓒ Ⓓ Ⓔ
12. Ⓐ Ⓑ Ⓒ Ⓓ Ⓔ
13. Ⓐ Ⓑ Ⓒ Ⓓ Ⓔ
14. Ⓐ Ⓑ Ⓒ Ⓓ Ⓔ
15. Ⓐ Ⓑ Ⓒ Ⓓ Ⓔ
16. Ⓐ Ⓑ Ⓒ Ⓓ Ⓔ
17. Ⓐ Ⓑ Ⓒ Ⓓ Ⓔ
18. Ⓐ Ⓑ Ⓒ Ⓓ Ⓔ
19. Ⓐ Ⓑ Ⓒ Ⓓ Ⓔ
20. Ⓐ Ⓑ Ⓒ Ⓓ Ⓔ
21. Ⓐ Ⓑ Ⓒ Ⓓ Ⓔ
22. Ⓐ Ⓑ Ⓒ Ⓓ Ⓔ
23. Ⓐ Ⓑ Ⓒ Ⓓ Ⓔ
24. Ⓐ Ⓑ Ⓒ Ⓓ Ⓔ
25. Ⓐ Ⓑ Ⓒ Ⓓ Ⓔ
26. Ⓐ Ⓑ Ⓒ Ⓓ Ⓔ
27. Ⓐ Ⓑ Ⓒ Ⓓ Ⓔ
28. Ⓐ Ⓑ Ⓒ Ⓓ Ⓔ
29. Ⓐ Ⓑ Ⓒ Ⓓ Ⓔ
30. Ⓐ Ⓑ Ⓒ Ⓓ Ⓔ

LSAT Writing Assessment Drill Answer Sheet

_____

_____

_____

_____

_____

_____

_____

_____

_____

_____

LSAT Practice Test Answer Sheet

SECTION 1

1. Ⓐ Ⓑ Ⓒ Ⓓ Ⓔ
2. Ⓐ Ⓑ Ⓒ Ⓓ Ⓔ
3. Ⓐ Ⓑ Ⓒ Ⓓ Ⓔ
4. Ⓐ Ⓑ Ⓒ Ⓓ Ⓔ
5. Ⓐ Ⓑ Ⓒ Ⓓ Ⓔ
6. Ⓐ Ⓑ Ⓒ Ⓓ Ⓔ
7. Ⓐ Ⓑ Ⓒ Ⓓ Ⓔ
8. Ⓐ Ⓑ Ⓒ Ⓓ Ⓔ
9. Ⓐ Ⓑ Ⓒ Ⓓ Ⓔ
10. Ⓐ Ⓑ Ⓒ Ⓓ Ⓔ
11. Ⓐ Ⓑ Ⓒ Ⓓ Ⓔ
12. Ⓐ Ⓑ Ⓒ Ⓓ Ⓔ
13. Ⓐ Ⓑ Ⓒ Ⓓ Ⓔ
14. Ⓐ Ⓑ Ⓒ Ⓓ Ⓔ
15. Ⓐ Ⓑ Ⓒ Ⓓ Ⓔ
16. Ⓐ Ⓑ Ⓒ Ⓓ Ⓔ
17. Ⓐ Ⓑ Ⓒ Ⓓ Ⓔ
18. Ⓐ Ⓑ Ⓒ Ⓓ Ⓔ
19. Ⓐ Ⓑ Ⓒ Ⓓ Ⓔ
20. Ⓐ Ⓑ Ⓒ Ⓓ Ⓔ
21. Ⓐ Ⓑ Ⓒ Ⓓ Ⓔ
22. Ⓐ Ⓑ Ⓒ Ⓓ Ⓔ
23. Ⓐ Ⓑ Ⓒ Ⓓ Ⓔ
24. Ⓐ Ⓑ Ⓒ Ⓓ Ⓔ
25. Ⓐ Ⓑ Ⓒ Ⓓ Ⓔ
26. Ⓐ Ⓑ Ⓒ Ⓓ Ⓔ
27. Ⓐ Ⓑ Ⓒ Ⓓ Ⓔ
28. Ⓐ Ⓑ Ⓒ Ⓓ Ⓔ
29. Ⓐ Ⓑ Ⓒ Ⓓ Ⓔ
30. Ⓐ Ⓑ Ⓒ Ⓓ Ⓔ

SECTION 2

1. Ⓐ Ⓑ Ⓒ Ⓓ Ⓔ
2. Ⓐ Ⓑ Ⓒ Ⓓ Ⓔ
3. Ⓐ Ⓑ Ⓒ Ⓓ Ⓔ
4. Ⓐ Ⓑ Ⓒ Ⓓ Ⓔ
5. Ⓐ Ⓑ Ⓒ Ⓓ Ⓔ
6. Ⓐ Ⓑ Ⓒ Ⓓ Ⓔ
7. Ⓐ Ⓑ Ⓒ Ⓓ Ⓔ
8. Ⓐ Ⓑ Ⓒ Ⓓ Ⓔ
9. Ⓐ Ⓑ Ⓒ Ⓓ Ⓔ
10. Ⓐ Ⓑ Ⓒ Ⓓ Ⓔ
11. Ⓐ Ⓑ Ⓒ Ⓓ Ⓔ
12. Ⓐ Ⓑ Ⓒ Ⓓ Ⓔ
13. Ⓐ Ⓑ Ⓒ Ⓓ Ⓔ
14. Ⓐ Ⓑ Ⓒ Ⓓ Ⓔ
15. Ⓐ Ⓑ Ⓒ Ⓓ Ⓔ
16. Ⓐ Ⓑ Ⓒ Ⓓ Ⓔ
17. Ⓐ Ⓑ Ⓒ Ⓓ Ⓔ
18. Ⓐ Ⓑ Ⓒ Ⓓ Ⓔ
19. Ⓐ Ⓑ Ⓒ Ⓓ Ⓔ
20. Ⓐ Ⓑ Ⓒ Ⓓ Ⓔ
21. Ⓐ Ⓑ Ⓒ Ⓓ Ⓔ
22. Ⓐ Ⓑ Ⓒ Ⓓ Ⓔ
23. Ⓐ Ⓑ Ⓒ Ⓓ Ⓔ
24. Ⓐ Ⓑ Ⓒ Ⓓ Ⓔ
25. Ⓐ Ⓑ Ⓒ Ⓓ Ⓔ
26. Ⓐ Ⓑ Ⓒ Ⓓ Ⓔ
27. Ⓐ Ⓑ Ⓒ Ⓓ Ⓔ
28. Ⓐ Ⓑ Ⓒ Ⓓ Ⓔ
29. Ⓐ Ⓑ Ⓒ Ⓓ Ⓔ
30. Ⓐ Ⓑ Ⓒ Ⓓ Ⓔ

SECTION 3

1. Ⓐ Ⓑ Ⓒ Ⓓ Ⓔ
2. Ⓐ Ⓑ Ⓒ Ⓓ Ⓔ
3. Ⓐ Ⓑ Ⓒ Ⓓ Ⓔ
4. Ⓐ Ⓑ Ⓒ Ⓓ Ⓔ
5. Ⓐ Ⓑ Ⓒ Ⓓ Ⓔ
6. Ⓐ Ⓑ Ⓒ Ⓓ Ⓔ
7. Ⓐ Ⓑ Ⓒ Ⓓ Ⓔ
8. Ⓐ Ⓑ Ⓒ Ⓓ Ⓔ
9. Ⓐ Ⓑ Ⓒ Ⓓ Ⓔ
10. Ⓐ Ⓑ Ⓒ Ⓓ Ⓔ
11. Ⓐ Ⓑ Ⓒ Ⓓ Ⓔ
12. Ⓐ Ⓑ Ⓒ Ⓓ Ⓔ
13. Ⓐ Ⓑ Ⓒ Ⓓ Ⓔ
14. Ⓐ Ⓑ Ⓒ Ⓓ Ⓔ
15. Ⓐ Ⓑ Ⓒ Ⓓ Ⓔ
16. Ⓐ Ⓑ Ⓒ Ⓓ Ⓔ
17. Ⓐ Ⓑ Ⓒ Ⓓ Ⓔ
18. Ⓐ Ⓑ Ⓒ Ⓓ Ⓔ
19. Ⓐ Ⓑ Ⓒ Ⓓ Ⓔ
20. Ⓐ Ⓑ Ⓒ Ⓓ Ⓔ
21. Ⓐ Ⓑ Ⓒ Ⓓ Ⓔ
22. Ⓐ Ⓑ Ⓒ Ⓓ Ⓔ
23. Ⓐ Ⓑ Ⓒ Ⓓ Ⓔ
24. Ⓐ Ⓑ Ⓒ Ⓓ Ⓔ
25. Ⓐ Ⓑ Ⓒ Ⓓ Ⓔ
26. Ⓐ Ⓑ Ⓒ Ⓓ Ⓔ
27. Ⓐ Ⓑ Ⓒ Ⓓ Ⓔ
28. Ⓐ Ⓑ Ⓒ Ⓓ Ⓔ
29. Ⓐ Ⓑ Ⓒ Ⓓ Ⓔ
30. Ⓐ Ⓑ Ⓒ Ⓓ Ⓔ

SECTION 4

1. Ⓐ Ⓑ Ⓒ Ⓓ Ⓔ
2. Ⓐ Ⓑ Ⓒ Ⓓ Ⓔ
3. Ⓐ Ⓑ Ⓒ Ⓓ Ⓔ
4. Ⓐ Ⓑ Ⓒ Ⓓ Ⓔ
5. Ⓐ Ⓑ Ⓒ Ⓓ Ⓔ
6. Ⓐ Ⓑ Ⓒ Ⓓ Ⓔ
7. Ⓐ Ⓑ Ⓒ Ⓓ Ⓔ
8. Ⓐ Ⓑ Ⓒ Ⓓ Ⓔ
9. Ⓐ Ⓑ Ⓒ Ⓓ Ⓔ
10. Ⓐ Ⓑ Ⓒ Ⓓ Ⓔ
11. Ⓐ Ⓑ Ⓒ Ⓓ Ⓔ
12. Ⓐ Ⓑ Ⓒ Ⓓ Ⓔ
13. Ⓐ Ⓑ Ⓒ Ⓓ Ⓔ
14. Ⓐ Ⓑ Ⓒ Ⓓ Ⓔ
15. Ⓐ Ⓑ Ⓒ Ⓓ Ⓔ
16. Ⓐ Ⓑ Ⓒ Ⓓ Ⓔ
17. Ⓐ Ⓑ Ⓒ Ⓓ Ⓔ
18. Ⓐ Ⓑ Ⓒ Ⓓ Ⓔ
19. Ⓐ Ⓑ Ⓒ Ⓓ Ⓔ
20. Ⓐ Ⓑ Ⓒ Ⓓ Ⓔ
21. Ⓐ Ⓑ Ⓒ Ⓓ Ⓔ
22. Ⓐ Ⓑ Ⓒ Ⓓ Ⓔ
23. Ⓐ Ⓑ Ⓒ Ⓓ Ⓔ
24. Ⓐ Ⓑ Ⓒ Ⓓ Ⓔ
25. Ⓐ Ⓑ Ⓒ Ⓓ Ⓔ
26. Ⓐ Ⓑ Ⓒ Ⓓ Ⓔ
27. Ⓐ Ⓑ Ⓒ Ⓓ Ⓔ
28. Ⓐ Ⓑ Ⓒ Ⓓ Ⓔ
29. Ⓐ Ⓑ Ⓒ Ⓓ Ⓔ
30. Ⓐ Ⓑ Ⓒ Ⓓ Ⓔ

LSAT Writing Assessment Drill
Answer Sheet